TOO FEW TOO FAR

THE TRUE STORY OF A ROYAL MARINE COMMANDO

GEORGE THOMSEN
AS TOLD TO MALCOLM ANGEL

AMBERLEY

This edition first published 2012

Amberley Publishing
The Hill, Stroud
Gloucestershire, GL5 4EP

www.amberley-books.com

British Library Cataloguing in Publication Data.
A catalogue record for this book is available from the British Library.

ISBN 978-1-4456-0620-0

Typesetting and Origination by Amberley Publishing.
Printed in Great Britain.

CONTENTS

ACKNOWLEDGEMENTS

My thanks go to A. Aquilina, D. Cory, S. McLeod, F. Mackenzie, and J. Monckton, for their invaluable input during the creation of this book.

GEORGE'S THOUGHTS

I would like to thank my good friend Malcolm Angel for putting pen to paper to create this book. Without his great efforts to get into the mindset of a Royal Marine Commando in time of conflict, and his patience with myself in making sure that all the jargon was correct, this story would just be my personal reminiscences of the men in my section NP8901 and the Marine detachment of HMS *Endurance* in April 1982.

When I look back over the years, there are a number of times when I have had a few close calls and I thought my number was up. None of these was more certain than back there in the Southern Hemisphere, where it all kicked off. A bizarre set of events or a twist of fate – call it what you will. For me it was a case of being in the wrong place at the wrong time.

When the shit hit the fan, Ladbrooks would not have given us good odds on coming out of this one, that's for sure. But you do what you have to do to win the day.

Against all the odds, we stepped up to the mark.

The history of the Royal Marines is testimony in itself. We were not the first, nor would we be the last.

From their creation in 1664, through to the present-day conflicts in Iraq and Afghanistan, the Royal Marines have done what they do, above and beyond expectations. For it is these actions that define who you are as a person.

George Thomsen

PREFACE

Some years ago it was my good fortune to meet George Thomsen, a former Royal Marine and a larger than life Northumbrian. After knowing George for several months I learnt that he had been more than a little involved in the South Atlantic War.

He talked of his experiences during the conflict and soon my interest became less conversational and more transfixed on his fascinating story.

What I was hearing was not an account of the struggle which took place on the Falkland Islands, but of a remote and desperate battle, played out against the backdrop of the rusty, derelict town of Grytviken on the shores of South Georgia. It was the story of an engagement of which I am ashamed to say I was only vaguely aware and, of which I knew precious little.

In fact, I soon found that there were indeed two battles on the far-flung frozen island: one to reclaim it as British territory, and the other (the first) in its desperate defence, in which George Thomsen had fought as a section commander.

This battle and the tension filled build up to it was an extraordinary contest between a handful of British Marines against the might of an Argentine invasion force. And it was a battle, fought with such grit and true British ingenuity that it resulted in the Argentines getting far more than a bloody nose, and resulted in an action unique in British military history.

It was a story that was begging to be written, and begins with George's arrival on the Falkland Islands nearly twelve months before the outbreak of hostilities. It is laid out before you now, not in the dry dusty language of the history book, but as seen through the eyes of a true Brit, by one who was there, by NP 8901 Royal Marine Commando George Thomsen.

The dialogue within the pages is not verbatim as it took place over twenty-five years ago.

MARCH 25th 1982

There was cold and there was this: a kind of cold that tunnelled deep down into your soul driving all memory of warmth screaming from your veins. It came at you from all sides, carried on the ice-filled wind; a wind which long ago had stung and numbed the flesh into submission. A wind ridden by the devil, slamming millions of tiny ice spicules, like barbed ice picks, into all in its path; chilling and freezing; deadly, and unrelenting.

I knew it well, I'd been here before, on other peaks, on other mountains, and other glaciers. It was what I was trained for, it was what I expected and it was what I had to endure. But this operation was off the scale, shit tough, make no mistake, it was pushing it to the limit.

The gale had been building for days. Even the *Endurance*, 2,200 ft below, hidden by the ridge to our backs, had groaned and tossed in the treacherous ice-filled waves as she rounded into the relatively calm waters off King Edward Point.

We'd chosen our post with care. On our lofty glacier with our camm'd Arctic windproofs and white tent straining on its ropes behind us, we were nigh on invisible from the sea but commanded a view across virtually the whole of our section of South Georgia. We knew already that this area had been the most tempting to the enemy and was the part that instinct and training told me would take the brunt of the impending invasion. This was long-awaited and could only come from one direction – the sea.

I swept the glasses round once more, from Stromness to Leith then to the Husvick harbours, miles apart and backed by high snow-covered ridges, making them virtually inaccessible from the frozen land; all three harbours now ugly and derelict shanty-towns of rusty tin roofs and drifting dunes of ice.

Nothing moved in Stromness and Husvick, apart from the odd elephant seal, now able to lie on the beach in relative safety since the abandonment of these once stinking slaughterhouses. There was nothing to see, with at least no danger to our tiny piece of empire. I was satisfied with that much at least.

Leith Harbour was a different story. The Argentine ship, the *Bahia Buen Suceso* riding the heavy swell at her quayside, was the reason we were here.

The radio crackled faintly and the tent flap opened behind me. It was the end of my shift. I pulled the glasses back up from the *Bahia Buen Suceso*, angled them towards the horizon, adjusted for distance and made one final sweep before sitting up.

It was Steve Chubb's turn to take the bins. He was kneeling beside me now, pointing at his watch.

"Anything?" He shouted. I read his lips rather than heard him.

"Thieving bastards are still working!" I shouted through cracked lips into the wind, then pulled the bins over my head and handed them across.

"Fuck-all out there either." I pointed in the direction of the raging ocean. "Should have no unexpected company tonight."

A strong squall carried my words away, but he clearly understood. If there were any more ships, they'd wait for calmer seas. I tried to return his grin as I headed for the relative warmth of the tent, but my face was too stiff with the cold.

Twelve hours later, in semi darkness, we were back down at the foot of the icy cliff. The storm was still tearing over the ridge of the glacier thousands of feet above, but we were warmed by the exertion and the fact that we were in the lee of the mighty edifice

Clouds of snow and ice had impeded our descent, the occasional squall and violent gust sweeping round the side and sometimes straight down, picking up the frozen white dust and blowing it from the ledges.

We waited now for the Wasp to pick us up. My Rolex told me it was a fag paper from 0600 hours.

In the dawn light it was soon clear that we weren't the only ones on the beach. Further down towards the water the shale was littered with life, all heads facing our way.

"Christ look at this lot, there's hundreds of 'em." Chubb scrunched down the beach.

"Yeah. May not all be seals though, Chubby lad," I shouted into the wind. I was more interested in scanning the horizon for our transport "Aye, could be sea lions and they'll have your fucking arm off if you get too close," I added.

"Now the bastard tells me." Chubb backed off fast, colliding with Laurie Church as an angry bull lunged at him. I guessed I was right – sea lions have no fear. You soon find out the difference when they go for you.

Giving up on my search of the horizon, I walked down the wet shale to join the two men. The smell where they were standing at the water's edge was intense, like a fishmonger's bin on a summer's day.

But there, up close in amongst the creatures, I could see that my guess had been wrong. The animal that had gone for Chubb was a leopard seal, a similar species and just as nasty, with two rows of razor sharp teeth.

Amongst them as they basked on the waters edge like shiny black stones, were the real monsters – the sea elephants. As we got closer, we identified them as the source of the smell, they were as rank as they were big. Weighing in at around four tons and maybe eighteen feet in length they showed no fear of us. It was as though we were being gracefully allowed an audience, in their space and on their beach.

I checked my watch "Best head back lads." I tapped the dial. It was 0614 and we needed to be back at the upper shoreline.

Two minutes later the Wasp came at us like a bat out of hell; an antiquated little killer, skimming the waves – rotors lower than the wet rocks as she burst into the tiny bay. Old but deadly, our transport was still a great little eradicator; flown by a pro, she'd be on you before you heard her and it was nice to know she was one of ours.

There'd be no burning and turning at this drop off and pick up, but it was obvious the pilot wanted to be on his way. I couldn't blame him. On the open beach he was a sitting duck. Like a giant insect the machine twitched, rotors thumping the air, wheels barely touching the beach, itching to be off.

I didn't want to be there any longer than I had to either, but the chopper had brought a new team and they needed to be briefed.

Within minutes I was climbing on board, the down draft trying to flatten me, and the wheels lifting off the deck before I'd slammed the door. Chubb and Laurie grinned, thumbs up through the racket chucked at us from the Rolls Royce powerhouse hammering above our heads.

It was going to be a helter-skelter ride, six feet max, hugging the coastline, pummelling through the wave-tops back to base.

I leaned back amongst the kit. After two days in the freezer the heat of the cab was hitting me big-time, like a mega anaesthetic.

We hurtled past the rocky entrance to the bay.

My head nodded.

The cold of the southern hemisphere had been chilling my bones now for nearly twelve months. All the while the dark clouds of anger had been building and looming over the Argentine mainland – the reason I had chosen to be here.

Now at last the rattling drums of war were nearing their crescendo. When they stopped the sky would break and the storm would begin.

My eyelids felt heavy. I fought the sleep that was coming down like a blanket and lowered my head.

CHAPTER 1

APRIL 1981:
NP 8901 HAVE LANDED

The turbofans of the VC10 changed their pitch and I eased myself round to look out through the oval window along the perfect symmetry of the swept wing.

Sunlight was glinting off the grey aluminium tip, now dipping below the horizon, as we altered our course.

Finally, the vast Atlantic had given way to the land that now spread out below me – sun baked and shade-less – under a perfect blue sky.

The four Rolls Royce 301 Conways altered their note again, and the change in gravity, as we levelled up then dropped down into the approach towards the Passo Carrasco, felt as though we had stood still in mid flight.

The change in note was welcome. 22,500 lbs of dry thrust times four equals a lot of noise, and the old RAF workhorse hadn't missed a beat since reaching her cruising speed in the cold and wet of the northern hemisphere.

Across the narrow fuselage all eyes turned towards the great city of Montevideo. Past the craning necks, I caught glimpses of skyscrapers in the city centre, hazy and discoloured beneath a mushroom of pollution, large shapes of ships in the great harbour, and the city stretching around the bay and beyond into the blur of the distant landscape.

The deep blue of the Atlantic that minutes before had seemed to go on monotonously for ever, was transformed beneath us now by a broad ledge of sand below the shallow water, which changed the sombre ocean into a brilliant blue before showing itself, white and inviting, separating the city from the sea like a glittering necklace.

Our flight path had powered us down the east coast of the Americas, before changing to 'south–north' on our approach across what the locals called the Rio de la Plata – better known to me as the River Plate, home to the first major naval action of the Second World War.

I'd watched the waters closely on the way in. OK, it was odds on I wouldn't see her, but it was worth a try. She was there, not far away. Three or four miles out from the shoreline, somewhere on the sea bed, sixteen thousand tons of German pocket battleship – the Admiral Graf Spee.

The citizens of Montevideo must have had a great free firework display, but not the captain and crew of the ill-fated ship. They say she stayed afloat burning for four days, after being scuttled by her own crew. What must have gone through their minds when they discovered the deception, and found that they'd done the Royal Navy's job for them through a brilliant piece of British Naval Intelligence bluff work.

Little wonder Captain Langsdorf blew his own head off.

I tried to picture what the Royals would have done in his position – hopelessly outnumbered and trapped from all sides – and guessed that that was where the bluff had been so brilliant. It simply wouldn't have worked against the Royals who would most likely have come out, full steam ahead, all guns blazing, and at least have rammed one of the enemy and taken them down with them.

It's called the Nelson spirit. If Langsdorf had that mindset, he would have called our bluff and soon have found that instead of the powerful force we had led him to believe were waiting for him, there were just three cruisers: Ajax, Cumberland and Achilles. The massive firepower of his battleship's guns would have blown them out of the water before they even got him in range.

Yes, it must have really pissed them off when they found out.

I thought about stifling a grim smile, but decided to avoid the cliché and turned my attention back to the view through the thick Perspex instead.

The view of the sea slipped by. I straightened my shoulders and eased my head from side to side feeling the click of stiff neck muscles.

The small stunted trees were much larger now, and I could see our shadow racing over small farm enclosures and low stone walls as we came in to land. Rubber burned and shrieked its greeting as we finally touched the airstrip, the massive tyres under the wings taking the weight first and cushioning the shock to the airframe, before the front two wheels gently kissed terra firma.

The belts tightened. Down at last, and slowing quickly from our terrific velocity, all four clam shells opened, increasing the roar from the turbofans to an even higher pitch, as they chucked everything, including the exhaust, into reverse thrust.

Dust swirled by my window. The RAF pilot retracted the clam doors, and the reinforced floor juddered as the disc brakes took over, quickly pulling us down to taxiing speed.

Swallowing, to release the pressure caused by the rapid change in thrust, I unbuckled the belt – now hanging limp in my lap – and looked round at the other guys. Opposite, Chubb and Hobbs, like passengers on a holiday flight, were reaching up for their gear.

"Here we are lads," one of the guys wise-cracked from the back, "From one shit hole to another!"

I guess he was looking out at the same scene as me – just dried up grass and a gaggle of untidy sheds on the distant perimeter.

"Yeah. Lousy bleeding service too. I'm still waiting for my fucking gin and tonic".

Naval Party 8901 had landed.

The heat and scent of the Uruguayan afternoon hit me as I emerged from the Jet's cool belly. The great expanse of runway reflected the heat as well as the light from the sun, which burned down mercilessly. I scanned the scene before us: the place looked like it had been cooked. It was a far cry from our departure at Brise Norton. I narrowed my eyes in the brightness, trying to get used to the glare, and heaved up my mountain of kit. Not all of it would fit into my Bergen and, like the others, my belts, pouches, personal gear, and all else essential to survival in the field, were draped about me.

With a small thud, the large cargo ramp scored a British dent in the field and the crew started to wheel down some of the heavy gear for the approaching wagons. A high-pitched diesel whine was announcing their presence, before they finally came into sight around the front of the jet, accompanied by the inevitable dust and acrid exhaust fumes belching out into the dry air. The sun had been busy hammering the cab roofs, which were stove hot as they shimmered in the heat when they bumped towards us. They finally pulled up beneath the tail plane of the VC10, which towered above them, casting its shadow like the fin of a great blue whale across the scene.

Squinting across the broad belt of dry grass, which separated the airstrip from the haphazard sheds, I picked out our coach which was due to follow the wagons to the docks.

Its doors and luggage bay hung open. The driver, idly leaning on the front nearside corner, made use of the only available shade.

We lugged the kit across and loaded up.

Once under way, the coach soon became an oven on wheels and, left with few options. I wearily leaned back in my seat to watch the changing scene outside the dusty glass. We were passing elegant palm trees strung out along the broad plazas of Montevideo. Their fronds hung limp in the still air, swaying languidly with our slipstream as we brushed past in the heavy afternoon traffic.

There had, at least, been a hot breeze from the high slits in the top of the windows, as we had motored through the suburbs, but even that small mercy had diminished, like our speed, now that we had reached the city centre. The coach was quickly becoming even hotter.

I watched the driver's reflection in his rear view mirror. The lucky bastard adjusted his Polaroid sunglasses and leaned back, straightening his olive-coloured arms on the wheel as the breeze, such as it was, wafted in from his wound-down window. I looked away, my wet shirt clinging uncomfortably to my back, and gazed out into the heat.

Horns echoed throughout the city as we stopped and started, while scooters dodged in and out like picadors in a bullring. Pretty girls in bright dresses sat at street cafés and slipped in and out of the stores while the pavements were busy with pedestrians.

The heat, the motion of the coach and the fatigue of the journey were beginning to drain me, and, as we bumped along, they worked their magic until, like some of the other guys, my head nodded and I began to doze. It was all a far cry from the cool summers of home, growing up in the terraced streets of Sunderland where the winters were cold enough for gravediggers to revert to jack hammers to dig the ground.

Dreams came and went, memories flitting with the motion of the coach, of service in Northern Ireland and the time, years before, when, against my father's will, I had joined up. He stood before me now in my dream as he had done in the train station, holding out to me the ripped half of a twenty-pound note. "When you come back lad," he promised as he tucked the other half into his top pocket, unsmiling – always unsmiling, "We'll have that drink."

"Fucking hell, look at that one." A shout from one of the lads woke me.

The coach had slowed, and a woman on the pavement outside our grimy windows had foolishly flashed a smile back up to one of the lads.

"Christ. Look at the tits on it, too!"

That was enough, we all woke up fast. The coach erupted with testosterone as everyone tried to catch a glimpse.

"Bloody 'ell driver. Stop the coach here!"

"Jesus. She'd look great under me!"

"Fuck off, I saw her first!"

The driver crashed his gears and tried to move on, his hand on the horn. I looked past the craning necks to where he was sat. OK, I couldn't read his thoughts in the rear view mirror, and anyway his eyes were hidden behind his shades, but I'd lay odds that he thought he had a coach load of monsters. And, who knows, he was probably right.

"Ere, yours is the one with dark hair, Jonesy!"

Raucous laughter.

"Fuck off!"

I turned back to the glass and caught a glimpse of the source of the excitement from between the bobbing heads. Hips swaying for our benefit, her black poodle on the end of a dainty pink lead, the smiling red headed girl slowly disappeared amongst the crowds of shoppers.

The traffic eased and we started to pick up speed once again, finally leaving the busy shops behind us. Soon we came to a grand and spacious square, surrounded by an area of large pillared buildings, where yellow and blue national flags hung as limp as the palms. Bright water shimmered in a fountain contained in a garden of emerald green, where a local hero, mounted in bronze, looked down from a great polished monolith of stepped marble. All around, the good citizens of Montevideo dotted the scene, criss-crossing the square as they went about their business, dwarfed by the buildings like busy ants.

A great shadow from the skyscraper bordering the square had lengthened with the day. It moved over the statue, before cutting indiscriminately across our path to shade the yellow stone walls of the city buildings just ahead of us. We drove briefly through its cool darkness and emerged back into bright sunshine, leaving the city centre and the colossus, with his frozen memories of past glory, behind us.

CHAPTER 2

HURRY UP AND WAIT

Half an hour later we were off the coach. I grabbed my Bergen, slung a strap over one shoulder, and took the ten paces to the concrete edge of the dock. The vehicles had disappeared from view among the grubby buildings, heading back towards the dockyard gates. Just their exhaust fumes remained, and the whining sound of their high-geared transmissions, gradually fading as they wound their way back to town.

I looked back at the other Marines who were extracting their kit from the pile of khaki which rose like a small hill on the dockside. But there was no rush so I returned my gaze to the harbour and listened to the water, chopping up and slapping against the rusting stanchions below my feet where the dock wall met the sea. It looked deep and oily at close quarters, not at all like the blue we'd seen from the air.

Merchantmen ploughed in and out of the central channel. Derricks lined the dockside, their pivoted arms swinging chained platforms into the bellies of the ships, and a nearby chimney sent up a dirty plume of smoke, which cut across the thin pink clouds, in the high stratosphere like a crazy Z from Zorro's sword. A lone gull wheeled over the water between me and a long mole which stretched far out into the deep harbour away on my left. I watched the bird, crying mockingly, as it dipped and rose with the currents of warm air, where the cooler sea met the sun-baked land.

The scene before me was typical of a working harbour. Only one thing was missing. The rusting iron bollards on our dockside, their shiny waists worn smooth by the constant motion from the heavy ropes of docked vessels, were clean and bare.

There was no fucking ship!

We were professionals and resigned to the fact that it happened (a lot). In fact I'd almost come to expect it as part of military life. We'd travelled thousands of miles and were dead on time. Now the powers that be had to get their act together. They knew we would play our part. We'd done our bit. We'd hurried up and got here. Now we just had to wait. After all, there was nowhere else to go, we were stranded on the dockside and the transport had disappeared! We had no choice.

Steve Chubb peeled off from the scrum and wandered over, throwing his kit down next to mine and sitting on it.

"Here we go again George," he said letting out a long sigh and folding his arms in resignation. I knew what was coming. It was on my lips. He said it for me.

"Hurry up and fucking wait!"

I sat down next to him, pulling my knees up to my chest, and grinned.

"Aye, you'd better believe it, Chubby lad. Another fucking balls-up."

The words "piss up" and "brewery" came into my head as I gazed out across the vast harbour.

A few of us, Steve Chubb included, had chosen to stick together after our tour of operations with 41 commando, in Northern Ireland. The nature of our work, where death or injury was a daily reality, brought us together in a bond known by soldiers the world over. A bond, which made us to want to stay together as a cohesive team. It wouldn't normally be possible, but we had earned by way of a preferential drafting the right to choose our next posting, which was a pleasant reward for our previous employment.

We chose The Falklands.

We would go together and would follow George Gill.

George was a kind of a father figure to us. He was a sniper with a career of combat behind him that included Borneo, and was greatly respected for his experience. He was also far and away the oldest of our team. He knew the Falkland Islands well and went back as often as he could to visit his two daughters and his former wife. George had told us about the hostile sabre-rattling from the Argentine mainland, and the vulnerability of the islands, and was concerned that one day soon there really would be an invasion. After all, it had always been on the cards and the Argies had never seemed so ready for a fight.

He wanted to be part of the tiny defence force stationed at Moody Brook, just below Wireless Ridge on the western extremity of Stanley Harbour, when it kicked off. The decision was made. We would go with him. It was that simple.

Now we waited patiently on the empty quayside. Our pre-embarkation training completed there were just under two score of us in total – codename NP 8901 Royal Marine Commando – heading south for a 12 month drafting to the Falklands. This name, as George had predicted, was the cause of great anger and resentment to the latest Junta now in charge of the nearby mainland – a fascist, right wing, 'bully boy' Junta, who called the islands the 'Malvinas' and saw them as theirs by right – a Junta whose preferred method of negotiation was 'extreme force.'

Little did we know that it was a Junta that we would one day be meeting.

I kicked a loose pebble over the edge and watched it disappear with a ripple into the oily scum. The sun's intensity had diminished and was now no more than pleasantly warm on my back. I scanned the harbour entrance once more for any sign of our transport then folded my arms, lowered my eyelids and waited.

Several hours of boredom later the sun was below the horizon, with just a faint afterglow remaining high up in the dark sky – just enough to see by and to illuminate the *Endurance*'s white superstructure, which towered above us as we finally, wearily, boarded ship. The red of the hull, made darker by the absence of the sun's rays, appeared black as she rolled very slightly in the deep waters where the estuary had finally given way to the great ocean of the southern hemisphere. The launch, still tied up, coughed and burbled as the exhausts dipped in and out of the salty brine which rose and fell in long slow waves, sucking along the side of the ship's welded plates. The smaller vessel had been our transport from the harbour, and had appeared as the cooler air from the ocean waters had begun to chill the concrete dockside. She had been a very welcome sight.

At this hour the heat of the day had long since gone and the ship's rail was cold and damp to the touch as I felt my way along it. With the others I was heading towards the iron mezzanine steps situated inside the main superstructure. Above me, three stories above, the line of bridge windows were lit yellow from within. Over them, bright navigation lights twinkled from the antennae mastheads, which rose another two stories in height again.

As I gazed up, a huge bird, darker than the sky, circled the ship briefly without moving its wings, then flew slowly away, dipping down towards the far shore, before finally disappearing into the gathering South American night.

We found the mess below deck. I moved quickly down the stairs – my size 11s squeaking on the patterned iron treads – and threw my gear on the best bunk left. I noticed that they had wooden sides, which didn't bode well; these were designed to hold you in, in rough weather, not for comfort. The faint vibration of the ship's engine was throbbing through the timber cot and the decking beneath my feet, and, as I sorted through my gear, this subsided into a rhythmic hum and the motion of the vessel began to change. Our skipper, Captain Barker was wasting no time.

We were once again under way, relentlessly heading south.

We would plough this course for the next four days, the steeply sloping curve of the *Endurance*'s reinforced bow cutting easily through the heavy swell. She wasn't a fast ship by any means, 13.5 knots maximum, but the powerful diesel two-stroke engine was not built to let you down. She had a 4000 miles range on a full tank, and that was enough for our purpose.

Our destination suited her well. We were heading for the kind of seas akin to her natural habitat. A few hundred miles south again and she would feel at home, but instead of the land of the polar bear she would be in the land of penguins.

The vessel had been born to roam the frozen waters of the northern hemisphere and was originally named The *Anita Dan*, before being bought and radically refitted by the Royal Navy. She was never built as an icebreaker but, nevertheless, could effortlessly push through the pack ice of the Norwegian Sea. As the *Anita Dan*, she was a Polar merchantman with freight in her holds, and paying passengers, cruising in some style in her elegant timber-panelled cabins. They sailed from her home in Denmark to Iceland, Greenland, and Spitzbergen, deep within the frozen Arctic Circle.

Avoiding icebergs was all part of a day's work and speed was not an advantage as she had gone quietly and efficiently about her business in the lonely oceans, far, far to the north of any normal shipping lanes.

We had acquired her back in the late sixties. The Senior Service needed a ship to take over from the tired old Falklands guard ship HMS *Protector* that was coming to the end of her useful life and the *Anita Dan* fitted the bill well; she just needed a few essential additions to help her fulfil her new role.

The navy needed a ship that could respond quickly in any given situation and Harland and Wolff were chosen to make the changes. Apart from the usual complete major refit, they built a great hanger behind the bridge and over the after-hold with a flight pad extending aft covering the old poop deck. The structure changed her shape radically, and when she finally left the dock, with her hull painted red, and the white ensign proudly fluttering in the breeze, she could discharge two Wasp helicopters, armed and ready with air-to-air and air-to-sea missiles.

She had completed her metamorphosis and was no longer the *Anita Dan* – she could carry a full naval crew, and a compliment of twelve Royal Marines. She was now the Royal Navy's brave new ship – Her Majesty's Ship *Endurance*.

"Pity we couldn't have seen her," I said, half to myself, leaning over the ship's rail, staring down at the dark ocean.

Now I was back up on deck the warm sea breeze smelt sweet and fresh. Together with the food in my belly, and a hot shower, it was working its magic. I could feel the weariness shrugging off me like a heavy cloak. Ozone, and the sound of the sea, was much better suited to a Sunderland lad than the oppressive heat of the earlier day.

The salt air reminded me of rare warm summer evenings, and the scent of the surf as it crashed and ebbed on the sandy beaches of Whitburn Bay back home.

"Lets face it, she could be bloody anywhere George," Hobbsie's cockney accent broke into my thoughts. I smoothed my moustache with the back of my hand and looked round at the. He'd stopped leaning over the ship's rail where he had been searching the impenetrable darkness of the sea below us.

"You daft bugger Tirpitz," he grinned, the scar – running from his mouth to his cheek – disappearing into his smile.

He was right of course. We'd passed somewhere near the grave of the Graff Spee miles back. I'd been told you could see her as you passed over – little chance in the dark, but there wasn't much else to do.

Steve Chubb straightened up from the rail on the other side of Hobbs and spat into the passing waves.

"Never mind the bleeding Graff Spee," he grumbled, "we should be back in Monte' chatting up the girls. That's where we should be."

Clamping his jaw shut and blowing down his pugilist's nose, he brought both palms down onto the steel rail with a metallic slap and squeezed, to emphasize his frustration.

"Ahh, never mind Chubby lad," I paused, "just be realistic." He looked like he needed a little reassuring. "You wouldn't have got a look in with me there anyway pal."

"Yeah, he's right mush," Hobbsie joined in, his grin half way up his teeth.

"Oh yeah, they like 'em big and ugly do they." Chubb's eyes flashed.

"I'd be beating 'em off with a stick man." I said.

"Dream on."

We resumed our position. Leaning on the cold rail and like the three wise monkeys, silently returned our gaze to the warm rolling sea.

We weren't inseparable, nor joined at the hip, but we had been together a long time, our friendship cemented years before in active duty – a Cockney, a Londoner from the better part of town, and a Geordie.

It was a strange cocktail, but it worked. We knew each other's strengths and weaknesses – we were a team. The banter never ended. No holds barred, piss taking from dawn to dusk. It kept me sane. Calling me 'The Tirpitz' was their idea of a joke. They thought it summed me up. The Tirpitz had been a giant WW2 German battleship – big, dangerous and only brought out when they knew they were in the shit. Well, Hobbs and Chubb liked it. I could live with that.

On the fourth day at sea, from our handrail on deck, we watched and waited until the first sight of the islands, appearing at first to be no more than a darker smudge on the horizon, came faintly into view.

The warm sea breezes were a distant memory, and the wind from the ocean was lashing at us, keen fresh and chilled, as though someone had left the freezer door open. Hardly surprising, we were 1150 miles south of the River Plate, and less than 400 miles from the edge of the winter sea ice that enveloped the vast frozen continent of Antarctica.

The day had started dull and got worse, becoming more overcast and wetter, cutting the visibility down by the hour. The islands remained indistinct as we closed in on them, their high mountain peaks hidden from us by banks of low sombre clouds.

I pulled up the heavy collar of my windproof smock as spray raddled the side of the superstructure, adding to the brine already soaking the wet decking. It stung my eyes and dripped in salty beads from the bristles of my moustache. It was supposed to be summer down here, but my 'head-over' – a warm woollen protection against the weather, stuffed somewhere in my Bergen – suddenly seemed like a good idea.

We had altered our course, probably for the first time since leaving the South American coastline. Rounding the eastern peninsular, we were now heading due west, directly towards Port Stanley.

The ship had dipped and rolled gently like a giant metronome throughout the last four days. Almost like a living creature, she had a rhythm of her own. Now that we had turned she faced a new ocean current but, once on a steady course again, she settled back down to her endless dance. Rigging slapped on the antennae masts and the ensign flapped gamely in the new direction of a brisk new wind.

In thirty minutes, and at a greatly reduced speed, we were nearing the narrow mouth of Port Stanley harbour. The waters were much calmer here. The land soon began to surround us, and the grey light from the wet clouds painted everything with a dull wash. Cold and wet, I cast my eyes around at the panorama as we plodded on. The lack of any high vegetation, or even a tree to break up the landscape, added to the marked difference between this place that we were now entering and our last sight of land.

Stanley was now dead ahead, the long concrete harbour scene drably reflecting in the ruffled water. A stretched-out row of buildings lined the front, with others from the town behind peeping between them through the little streets that ran back up the sloping shoreline, as if trying to catch a glimpse of the water. A look of despair and neglect seemed to pervade the entire scene.

My shoulders dropped, and Hobbs kicked the steel plate of the ships rail, perfectly in tune with my thoughts.

"Christ". I looked at Chubby and Hobbs. "We've dropped a fucking bollock here and no mistake."

"Sod it".

"Shit".

Their replies summed up my thoughts to the letter.

I thrust my hands deep into my pockets and flashed a look towards the bow. The near silence had been shattered by the heavy rattle of the ship's anchor chain. I watched as it clanged and bucked wickedly along the deck, before spewing out from the bow, its speed of passage undiminished as the 12 tonnes of Danish iron at its head, freed from its shackles, disappeared in a white plume beneath the surface.

As the noise of the anchor's passage ceased, an untidy flock of gulls wheeled in raucously from the land. They circled overhead, mocking us with their cries, before settling in untidy rows along the high rigging. Some of them looked down at us curiously, chattering; others shifting from one leg to the other like high wire artists, gave forth great scornful yells, for all the world like they were taking the piss. Across the water bodies and vehicles were making ready to get us ashore. Slowly the reality of the situation was sinking in. This island would be our home for at least twelve months.

"Bollocks." I breathed through my teeth, and met Hobbs's eyes. Had we come half way round the world for this? He was leaning against the wet superstructure, head on one side, eyebrows raised, mouth firmly shut in a wide gash. He didn't need to speak. He just filled his cheeks with little pockets of air and looked at me ironically.

Chubby was next to him "Great" he breathed out in a long sigh, finishing in his trademark macabre chuckle. "What do we do now then men – bloody swim!?"

He had a point, we were still a hundred yards from the quay, and it was 'hurry up and wait' time again – with no sign of any means to get us to the shore.

Eventually our transport showed, indistinctly at first then quite clearly heading in our general direction, chugging slowly out from the dockside.

She was the MV *Forest* – a small cargo vessel. I found out later she belonged to the Falkland Islands' Government. I guess that's why she was like a miniature *Endurance*, painted red with a white superstructure. It made sense really. You'd want to see her easily if she got stuck in the floating winter pack ice. There's not much else big and red in the frozen waters of Antarctica; it was twenty years since the last whaler had towed in its bloody prey.

Fifteen minutes later I'd clocked her skipper's broad pink face. He'd lumbered onto the deck behind his bridge after bringing his little ship alongside; a big man, with hairy arms and hands, weathered pinkish red, like his swollen face. He looked tired and bleary eyed as he shepherded us on board.

Eventually we cast off and made our way steadily towards the quay. I'd chosen to stand in the bow of this new transport. From there I could see across the heads to where we were going and had a good view of the rust-streaked bridge behind me. As my eyes swept over the superstructure I caught sight of the skipper's flushed face. It was close up to the inside of the bridge window. I did a double take and looked back again, but this time with more interest.

He had the look of a man trying to see through a fog. That was worrying. One of the lads had named him the "Big Plonker". When I looked back towards the quay – which was getting alarmingly close – it seemed that the name would fit.

He had misjudged our speed by a mile, but we kept on ploughing through the water without showing any sign of slowing. Grabbing the rigging at the foot of the boom with my right hand, I wrapped the heavy rope around my forearm and braced myself for the inevitable.

I wasn't the only one who'd noticed.

"I say chaps, do you think we might be going a little fast," shouted Chubby.

His laugh was lost amongst other cries of derision.

"Oi! We're not fucking water skiing you daft twat!"

"Plonker!"

"Speed it up!"

They always say that road accidents, crashes and the like seem somehow to happen in slow motion. Well that's true, you can take it from me. I've been in a few of those spots – you know, heads you win tales you die. Your mind, quite simply, works on a faster plain. It's a survival thing. OK, this wasn't one of those occasions, far from it, but the same gear change was taking place none the less.

The deck bucked beneath my feet as we struck, my ears filling with the sound of iron plate scraping on timber and concrete, crunching and mangling with the force of our impact, as our momentum tortuously dragged us along the unyielding sea wall.

Swinging on the rope, I watched the party on the quay as we scraped along. The moment we struck, they all took a step back, like sequence dancers who had forgotten to smile. Open-mouthed, their heads turned and their eyes followed our grinding progress, until we finally stopped thirty feet down the jetty.

Acrid, hot tasting white exhaust was still spewing out from the funnel, like a sea mist, drifting across the deck. It made the whole thing surreal, akin to a scene from a Dunkirk war movie. The silence that followed was our cue. The tension broke, I breathed out and joined the others in a huge ironic cheer, echoed, seconds later, by the Marines on the quay.

"Hells teeth, Tirpitz. Is this a sodding omen?" Chubby rubbed a bruised ankle.

"Why aye, man." I answered, but was busy looking down the quayside in the same direction as Hobbs. "Things will probably get worse from now on lad... Here, don't we know those two geezers Hobbsy?"

Hobbs was watching the two men I'd noticed. They had broken away from the jeering welcoming party, and were now heading towards us, carefully scanning the faces on the deck.

It was Ginge and Dan from our old unit, 41 Commando, and they were looking for us.

The evil grins on their faces, when they clocked us, said it all.

"Welcome to our island paradise," drifted wickedly up from the side of the quay.

CHAPTER 3

IN COLD BLOOD

I leaned on the sill, with the cold air chilling my knuckles. Dawn was over, but it was not yet sun-up and the scene outside was bleak. A brisk wind was catching the tops of the little mounds of un-grazed tussocks of grass just outside the window, before gusting down towards the sodden ground in the distance, ruffling the brown stalks between the grey boulders like ripples on a lake.

In the background, the twin peaks of the Two Sisters dominated the horizon, the faint tinge of green in the lower stalks of grass becoming lost with the distance, everything blurring into grey and brown like an old sepia photo. It was bleak in the extreme.

Letting the curtains fall back, I rubbed my eyes and turned towards the door, closing it quietly behind me so as not to wake the two other men in the room.

I was still missing the motion of the ship and had woken early to the quiet of the barracks. Still, I figured, it was good to be awake. The OC wanted to see me later, so today could be important. My mind travelled back to the last exercises on Dartmoor when I'd had my chance to show that I could lead a section. It all seemed a world away now. I'd come through the training, but would they promote me now or not? I'd waited long enough to find out. I looked at my watch – two more hours and the waiting would be over.

The cold outside in the corridor bit through my tee shirt, making me shiver involuntarily. I guess that the three bodies in our cramped quarters had turned the temperature up a notch. Not that I was complaining. It was a strange billet, a crappy concrete block outside, but inside it wasn't half bad. There was carpet on the floor, and a light-shade and curtains. In fact, our room would have been at home in a cheap motel. I guess maybe it was an attempt to make the year's posting a little more bearable.

I turned right at the next corridor, opened the outside door that led to the gym, and stepped out. If I'd thought it was cold in the corridor I was wrong. The Antarctic wind, blasting in from the near frozen ocean, had met no obstacles since leaving its kingdom of ice. The first thing it hit was the shoreline of the creek just beyond the gym, the second was me. It slammed into me like a frozen train.

The next day found me heading back to Stanley, but the reasons why I was being sent were still not clear to me. We had taken the long-wheel-base Land Rover and we were now bucking along the narrow track into town, its tough all terrain tyres and rigid suspension not giving an inch to the rutted surface. Predictably, Chubby and Hobbs had been taking the piss since I'd finally got promotion, and getting my own driver had them rolling around. Like true mates they would probably try a bit of ganging up now, so I'd promised myself I'd keep a few steps ahead. From what I'd heard from the 'grunts' going home, it might help to alleviate the boredom.

I looked across the cab at the driver, a few years younger than me, and hanging on to the wheel as we manoeuvred round one of the bigger pot-holes.

"You know where it is then?" I shouted as he crunched into third. I could see his brain working

"Yeah. I reckon." He shouted back without taking his eyes off the track. "Can't miss it, they said, straight down the road – big white building with a blue lamp, just past the little church."

He snicked the lever into fourth and grinned at the road.

"They reckon nothings fuckin' more than about 10 miles away anyway."

"You'd better believe it." I shouted across the cab, remembering what George had told me on the trip down. "The only roads are in town and there's sod all of that. Everything else is strictly off-road pal!"

We jolted over a pothole, the steering wheel juddering between his hands.

"Should come in handy then," he shouted, slapping the wheel.

We had woken to a cloudless morning and, despite the biting wind, the sun was warming the cab, so I slid back the side window and hung my arm out, curling my fingers round the galvanised rain gutter for support. The chilled salt air blasted my arm but the steel was still warm to the touch, from where the vehicle had been standing in the compound. Crashing down another rut, I tightened my grip on the seat belt, and turned my head towards the open window. A flock of gulls were racing across the choppy waves between the horizon and the shoreline just twenty yards on our left.

I didn't need the cold air in my face to bring my mind into focus on the little church. We had passed it soon after leaving the docks. It had stood behind a neat little hedge – a white weatherboard building with a little stunted bell tower and red tin roof. It was the first landmark I'd seen on our route out of town to the barracks. My eyes had taken note in the dim light and I'd logged it subconsciously.

We rocked along a few more miles, the town ahead of us slowly rising into view. I'd soon be seeing the church again and the police station, if it was next door like they said it was. I wouldn't be going into the church – they were places for other people – but apparently I'd be spending some time in the station. It would have been nice to know exactly why. The reason for my visit hadn't yet made a lot of sense.

I thought back to my meeting the day before, and puzzled over my strange instructions.

"Oh, bye the way, we've got a job for you tomorrow, Corporal Thomsen." Sergeant Major Noone had collared me after I'd been made up.

"Sergeant Major." I stood at ease a few feet from his desk.

"Yes," he said slowly, looking down at the papers in front of him. He slid them to one side, carefully putting a folder on top, before lining them up at the corner as though they were of great importance.

"Yes," he repeated leaning back in his seat. "We've got a job for you in town. In the police station to be precise." He reached out his right hand and drummed twice with two fingers on the folder. "They've asked us to help. Seems their sergeant needs to be somewhere else tomorrow. Bit short handed apparently." He repeated the tattoo. "So we're sending you down to do a spot of babysitting." He paused. "They've got a guy in the cells. Just need someone responsible to sit with him for the day." He glanced up, his mouth a parody of a smile. "He shouldn't give you any trouble."

"Sergeant Major?" I said, loaded with questions.

Breathing out he pulled the papers back towards him and lifted the edge of the file, studying the printed page beneath before giving me a little more information.

Two minutes later, after finishing the briefest possible explanation of my task, he looked back up from his desk, seemingly surprised at my raised eyebrows.

"Oh, we'll be sending you down some grub George, got to keep your strength up. Can't have you passing-out with hunger." He picked up his pen and looked at me, like he was wondering why I was still there.

"That's it corporal, you can fall out." It was an order.

"Sergeant Major." I left the room with him studying the papers as though I had already gone.

But that was yesterday. The squeal of the Rover's brakes broke into my thoughts and dragged me back to present – we had arrived at our destination. I climbed down from the vehicle and stood in front of the Police Station.

They were right. You couldn't miss it. The union flag straining at the top of the high white pole was a dead give away. It slapped in the chill breeze.

The smell of the Rover's exhaust fumes had left the car park, but I could still hear her motor rising and falling with the gear changes, as she slowly trailed away into the distance. Gulls began to call from the harbour water just the other side of a green space between the station and the sea. Their screams helped to kill off the sound of the departing vehicle; my boots scrunching on the compacted grit finished the job.

The place even looked like a nick, big functional and square, and, like the little wooden church next door, it had British Empire Colonial Building running through it like a stick of Blackpool rock.

The desk sergeant looked up as I let the heavy black door swing to behind me. Likely he hadn't heard the vehicle – the door and windows looked like they'd been built to keep out the natives. Inside felt solid and calm and smelt of wax polish.

"Thomsen?" he said looking down at his papers and then back to me.

"Aye?" I said, admiring his razor sharp powers of deduction. "Seems I'll be spending the day with your guest."

"Yep, that's the general idea. We're grateful you could help," he said, dropping the flap of the desk and leading me through the back to the cells. The way he said it you'd have thought it was my idea.

"No problem pal, what's he like?"

"Len?" He thought, crumpling up his mouth. "Nice bloke."

And he was. In fact, after I took the place of the 'uniform' who had nodded thankfully when he left the cell, we got on just fine. Len was just an ordinary grey-haired guy that I'd put somewhere in his fifties.

We talked to pass the time and I learned a bit about the islands from him. Then we got to talking about news from home. He was keen on that, which I guess was only natural as I learned that he would soon be travelling across the oceans to spend the rest of his natural life on British soil.

I watched him as he spoke, moving very little, sitting neatly on his bunk and leaning back against the cold grey wall.

He had an air of dignity and calm as though completely at ease with his fate.

After all, there was no doubt of his guilt. He had committed murder. The fact that his crime was in broad daylight and on his neatly edged front lawn hadn't helped his case much either. It had been a deliberate act of slaughter and he gave the impression of being quite satisfied with the result. Len, I found, had no intention of covering his tracks.

It was only later that I learned about the rumours of infidelity which on occasion had ebbed and flowed in an undercurrent of gossip around the islands. But this was all news to me now as I sat opposite him on the only chair in the cell, and listened.

Len's offence had been a true crime of passion. Fanned by pernicious chit-chat? True or false? I never found out, but he had believed his wife to be guilty of some form of perfidy. He had tried and convicted her in his own mind before exacting his own cruel execution.

Brandishing a filleting knife, he had dragged her from the house onto the front lawn, where he had forced her onto her knees before slitting her throat from ear to ear.

A chill ran down my spine as the walls of the cell closed in around me.

The sun had dipped well below the horizon by the time I heard the sweet music of the returning Rover. I heard the door slam in the car park and the scrunching of boots through the high open window and was glad of it. The cell had become claustrophobic and grey, the only light coming from the bulkhead lamp on the ceiling. You can guess that I was more than ready to leave and, as I swapped places with the sergeant and said my farewells to Len, it occurred to me that I'd only really come into contact with two locals so far.

One rammed boats, and the other was a cold-blooded killer.

CHAPTER 4

HEARTS AND MINDS

Slowly, imperceptibly slowly, the twin peaks of the Two Sisters mountains rose above the horizon. The four of us had been heading towards them for sixty minutes since leaving Moody Brook and as yet seemed hardly to have closed the distance. It was of course an illusion – one I had seen before – a trick mountains played, and not exclusive to the Falklands. Trouble was, like all gags, if you hear them more than once, the joke begins to wear thin. Still, I told myself, the sweat prickling my body was proof enough of our progress. It called for a break, and it was right time to vent-off.

We stopped on a dry-ish patch of ground. The two ruts which had cut deep on either side of our route, showing where the last vehicle had fought its way through, had ceased twenty minutes back down the track, and the ground had been worsening the further out we got, becoming wetter and boggier between the tough little hillocks of tussock grass.

It had been hard going, but we were making good time and could afford to make the essential stop. I slipped off my tightly packed Cyclops Rock Bergen and let it fall carefully onto a dry patch of shale. The other three guys did the same, the radio operator gratefully lowering his forty pound burden with a curse. I made a note that we'd share the weight from now on, each taking a turn of a few hours for the next five days of slog.

Arctic windproofs do what their name implies; they have big buttons that frozen fingers can close and open, and a zip keeping in the heat. Lifesavers when the temperature plummeted, but literally deadly to the amateur.

We slipped them off and pulled off our green ribbed jumpers. Mine felt damp to the touch and it had to dry. I folded it neatly and stashed it just under the top flap of my Bergen. The sun disappeared behind another fast moving cloud and the steady cold wind whipped through my shirt. It was the body heat and sweat that were the killers. If we didn't dry and the temperature dropped, wind proof or not, the damp clothes underneath would freeze. Hypothermia is a nasty way to die.

Five minutes later, windproofs back on, we set off again. I wanted to be in the lea of the Two Sisters before we stopped for some grub and a wet, and I guessed that could take another three hours. The ground had become impassable; we were on foot now and as we progressed, the patches of dry between the bog were becoming scarce. Pools of stagnant water and oozing peat soaked my German Para boots, at times coming over the top, darkening the khaki of my denims. But at least we were cooler now, and our upper bodies dry.

The hours passed and, with a curse, I sunk deeply once again into a patch of ground that I thought would take my weight. My boot came out of the mud with a sucking noise, stinking of rotting vegetation. Just ahead, I could see the ground rising. We had been skirting the foot of the Sisters for the last few minutes and the higher ledge I was heading for looked welcoming. I looked at my watch it was a good time to rest and eat.

The tussock grass preferred the dryer stony terrain, growing taller and in larger tufts, and, although the wind was constant and part of the islands make up, closer to the ground with your back to the little hillocks there was shelter. We sat here, grateful for the relative calm, with just the sound of the tall stalks whispering and clicking above our heads.

"Where are we George?" It was Brum Holden. I'd pulled out the map and not for the first time was trying to judge the distances and decipher the landmarks. My Bluey – a tiny gas cooker – was hissing, the flame changing note and popping when the wind sneaked through.

"I reckon we are about here Brum," I said holding out the page and stabbing a finger.

"Fucking hell. Call that a map?"

I didn't, but it was all I had.

"Where's the bleeding grid?"

The flame roared its little protest as the wind made a concerted effort.

"You tell me," I said, turning the chart over and searching once again for any sign of reference. "They even forgot the scale when they made this one."

I carefully slid it back into my pocket and patted it ironically. Jock Milne and Bob Fenson looked up at this but said nothing. They were already eating their grub.

It was "babies heads" again. Some kind of dumplings and meat; we hoped it was minced beef but you couldn't tell. Whatever it was, it kept you alive. I pushed the splodge around in the tin and watched it bubble.

The map was rubbish, but the landmarks on our route were unmistakeable. I took a mouthful and looked across at the huge bulk of Mount Kent, her top sliced off by fast clouds. After we had rounded her base, the next sighting would be Mount Estancia. With her on our right we would make our first destination, Estancia House, by sundown.

I took another mouthful and looked back the way we had come, narrowing my eyes into the wind, which carried the song of a moorland bird, and I caught a brief sight of the creature, brown and speckled, flying low between the waving grasses before disappearing from view.

The great ridge on our left, that had kept us company for the last few miles, darkened on its pale grey surfaces and turned black in its deep secret crevasses as cloud after cloud sped across it in the relentless battering wind. My chart called it Goat Ridge but, with its long backbone of jagged rocks carved over millions of years into fantastic shapes, it looked to me more like the armour-plated back of a stegosaurus.

I cleaned out my tin and brought my mug up for a wet. The Harry Black Maskers felt familiar, bringing back memories of frozen OPs. The strong sweet liquid was still near boiling; without the tape the tin would have removed a few layers of skin. I wiped the rim, stood the mug down on a flat piece of shale and half closed my eyes. We could afford another fifteen minutes.

Although we had been here now for three weeks, this was our first patrol. We worked on a three-week rota: camp duties, training and patrols. I'd sent half the team out in the first week, the Beaver flying them to the south of the island, before starting their patrol on foot. Now it was our turn, with no Beaver, but if we got offered a lift part way on from any of the scattered homesteads that would suit us just fine. With that thought I reached across to my pack, feeling the shape of the Scotch bottle in the bottom, reassuring myself that it was still intact. With our 'duty free' we could afford the odd gift and whisky was always a good persuader.

As we sat in the shelter of the tall grasses the sun decided to crack through the higher grey murk, bringing as it came an instant heat to the thin southern hemisphere air. It was as though a brief and dramatic scene change had taken place, our previously drab cloud-covered surroundings now lit with an eerie and wild beauty. It felt good, like being back home on Dartmoor. I stretched my legs, tipped my beret forward and leaned back on my mound of grass.

We would soon be staying with our first islanders and my thoughts went back to my conversation with Ray in the mess on the night of the first Patrol's return to base.

"And here's something to think about George" Ray had been filling me in on their week out. I put down my glass. "Go on."

"Well you know about the lad that went missing?"

Yeah, I knew. Ginge had told me soon after our arrival. "Alan Addis. Last August. Eighth, I think. Have you heard something then?" I was interested.

"I don't know. Could be." He took a pull at his drink. "We'd been chatting up some of the local birds, at the settlement. We'd had a good time the night before. You know what its like. Having a bit of a laugh like. Anyway in the morning we were just off when I overheard this local talking to one of the girls in the kitchen."

"Yeah. What?"

"He was telling her to wind her neck in and told her that unless she wanted to see a repeat of what happened at North Arm she'd better keep well away from any

Marines." He looked at me and pulled a wry face. "Sounded like a right nasty piece of work. Strange that, the guys had seemed alright the night before." He picked up his empty glass and, pushing his chair back with a scrape, walked across to the noisy crowd at the bar.

Rumours again. The island was full of it. It seemed to be that kind of a place. Like I said, I'd already heard the craic, and it wasn't good. The fact is Royal Marine Commando's don't just disappear.

Allan Addis was part of the patrol that had gone to North Arm last year. The settlement is in the south of the island on a narrow strip of land between Falkland Sound and the Bay Of Harbours. Our friend the captain had taken them down in the MV Forest, mooring up in the clear icy waters of the bay. They had stayed overnight, and the first time anyone in the patrol knew that they were a man down was at stand-to in the morning.

At first no one was overly concerned. OK he was in trouble for missing roll-call but Marines had been known to turn up a little late after a night out. Annoying, but no real problem. I could imagine the craic from the lads over breakfast on the 'Forest', probably hoping that he'd stayed over with a girl in the settlement. God he was in for some stick when he finally turned up. I could picture it. They'd have been lining up for him.

Trouble was he didn't and it wasn't long before amusement started to turn into concern.

As the morning wore on they began to look for him. When they found that he wasn't at the settlement they searched everywhere, combing the entire area for any sign of him.

It was inexplicable. They could find not one trace of him anywhere.
Soon every crevice, bog and ditch in the wretched frozen land around the settlement were probed and searched, and then searched again.

Alan Addis was fit, strong and trained in Arctic warfare and survival and, although August was still midwinter with temperatures at night dipping well below zero, he would have been better trained than most to survive. But it still didn't answer the question. He couldn't just vanish – there at least had to be a body.

Soon after my arrival on the island I'd met the diver who had searched the bay. He had found nothing. An expert, he knew how to read tides and currents and assured me that if the Marine had have fallen into the bay he would have been found. He could not have been washed out to sea but would have remained in the bay. With its rocky banks and crystal clear water he simply could not have been missed.

As the days went by some of the guys had come to their own conclusion as to his possible fate. And on the basis that Royal Marines look after their own, the armoury had been locked and all patrols cancelled.

Eventually, a team arrived from Scotland Yard, but they also turned up nothing, leaving the island with the case still open.

Alan was never found.

With this past history in mind I passed on Roy's over-heard threat to the 2 I C.

Hauling my thoughts back to the present, I snapped the clip on my webbing and pulled up my collar. The clouds and wind were winning their ceaseless battle, extinguishing the sun's brief visit and the colour had once more drained from the land. We had at least four and maybe five more hours slog and then the short day would be closing on us fast. Leaving the stony clearing with no trace of our stop, we bent once more virtually head on into the strengthening breeze.

My SLR had felt cold to the touch when I raised it, the residual warmth from my hands having left during our short break. But now a few miles on with the weapon held out in front of me, moving from side to side as I kept balance on the rough ground, the wooden stock returned the heat. Dull light reflected off the polished wood and the black steel of the barrel and caught like crescent moons in the three hole flash eliminator. I gripped the weapon and swung to the right as I slid awkwardly on a wet tuft. The rifle felt reassuring and familiar and on patrol never left my hands.

I jinked across a dry boulder and scrambled down the other side, empty strap hooks for and aft swung with the movement. SLRs were good but I rated this one as a bit special. An older model, made with great precision, it was a satisfying reassurance that the 7.62mm rounds slung underneath in their black mag went where you aimed them. She had been zeroed in with great care and I liked that.

High up, two Upland Geese traversed the blustering sky, moving fast with the advantage of the wind, their passage had been camouflaged by the bulk of Mount Kent. I hadn't noticed them until they left its darkness, their distant calls drifting across the vast open space between the gusts. The pair's appearance made me aware that at last the mountain had shifted. Its huge bulk had loomed on our left for hours and seemed immoveable, as though we were on an endless treadmill, getting nowhere. But now, as I studied its new shape, I judged that the cap hidden beneath the greyness was around nine o'clock and we were at last beginning to leave its rocky base. Turning back into the wind and searching the sky, I just caught sight of the two dots as they blended in to the rising mass of Mount Vemet filling the horizon the other side of the vast valley of space between the hidden peaks. It was time to stop again briefly, the land was beginning to slope away, looking dryer on the long final leg down to Estancia and it was my turn to shoulder the radio.

"Hey George!" Brum shouted across, wiping his brow with his right sleeve, his hand still wrapped around his pistol grip. "They reckon that if you don't like the weather here, just wait ten minutes and it will change". He looked up at the sky in case I hadn't noticed.

"About time," I threw back, following his glance and keeping up the steady pace. We were an hour in to the last leg.

He was kind of right. The wind had all but dropped and the low late afternoon sun had finally broken through, looking for all the world, as though it were here to stay.

The scudding clouds that had dogged us all day had been replaced in minutes by high cumulus that towered up into the stratosphere, leaving the snow capped peaks of the mountains below them, at last clearly visible. I blinked; the blue sky – so rich it hurt your eyes – picked out the scene in minute detail.

The ten minutes bit was a bit fanciful but I could see the reasoning behind the words. It was like we had been transported to another place.

Sheep had begun to appear on the horizon; the outriders of the flocks watched us curiously as we silently padded on, our rubber-soled boots making no sound on the surface of the gentle slope. Short, well cropped grass covered the ground around us, its green-ness broken only by the odd tufty hillock and occasional islands of rock, crowned by outcrops of yellow flowering gorse. Behind us our shadows stretched for yards on the smooth green velvet, while the mountain tops and clouds, the colour of molten steel, bore witness to the stunning sunset.

Our pace quickened now and became lighter. The house had come into view. First a few rooftops and chimneys poking above the horizon, joined together indistinctly in a mass, all painted the darkest burgundy; the red wriggly tin, shaded in deep gloom, by the sinking sun. As we neared, with the ground falling away before us, we stopped and took stock. The buildings stood not more than a hundred yards distant. I saw the figure of a man leave the darkness of the porch and come towards us, his shadow preceding him like a giant.

He reached us, smiling, his right hand outstretched in friendship. Behind him the sun was all but set, bouncing red fire off the mirror smooth water of the creek behind, and framing the farm buildings in perfect silhouette. A young woman came out and stood to one side of the house cradling a baby.

"Hearts and Minds," I thought. Let's do it. And, holding my rifle in my left fist, shook the outstretched hand. "Tony Heathman?" I enquired. His grip was firm.

"Dead on time gentlemen," came the reply. "Welcome to Estancia."

CHAPTER 5

ROUND THE TABLE

Carrying my kit, I ducked through the wide farmhouse door, following Heathman into the scrubbed kitchen. Brum and Jock tagged in with me while Bob filled the doorway, pulling off his beret, taking in the big comfortable room. Pots and pans hung from a bar by the range and a heavy pine table stood on the timber floor filling the centre. Chairs were drawn up close, apart from one nearest to the cooker, which faced us sideways on, where it had been pulled back. A baby's bib lay on the seat, its ribbons dangling over the side, one nearly reaching the floor, the other draped on the spindle between the two side legs.

I could see what Tony had meant in his greeting – the table was laid and I was already salivating with the smell of the roast.

He picked up the bib and walked across to the open door in the far wall. I could see a hallway and stairs, with the last rays of sun coming from a window somewhere, blasting a long thin stripe through the wallpaper.

"Ailsa's just gone to put the baby down," he said, looking up towards the ceiling. "Best keep the noise down."

We'd said our brief hellos to her outside the porch whilst she smiled up at us rocking the well wrapped bundle. We made all the right noises looking into the little round hole in the shawl at the tiny features. Luckily the baby was asleep so she was spared the coochi coos and funny faces.

"I guess you'll want to get cleaned up before dinner," Tony carried on. It was a statement.

"I hope you guys are hungry." He looked at Jock who sniffed the air like one of the Bisto Boys. Jock's rangy figure and lean face hid the fact that he could eat for Scotland.

"Just lead me to it, man, and I'll do my best".

"Come on then," Tony scanned his watch grinning, "I'll show you your room." I flicked up my wrist and checked the dial. It was seven o'clock, near as damn it.

"Shall we say twenty past?" he said, looking at me.

"Aye, right. It's your house, man, and your rules. I reckon we can hold out another twenty minutes but half an hour, mind, would be pushing it." We laughed softly and, lugging our kit into the hallway, followed him quietly up the stairs.

"Sit anywhere you like," Ailsa called across from the range, half turning to look at us as we came back down. We didn't need encouraging – chairs scraped enthusiastically across the floorboards. Above the table, a single bulb in its china-man's hat was casting a warm glow, throwing bands of light on the drawn red and white curtains. After the clattering of wood I could hear the wind had got up again; it was busy trying to find a way past the glass barriers of the windows.

Despite the warmth of the room, I pulled up the collar of my shirt. The cosy house belied the vicious temperature drop that I knew was taking place outside. It came hand in hand with the darkness and the bitter, early winter winds that would blast their way up from the icy waters of the nearby creek.

Ailsa stood behind me at the oven. She wiped her hand down her apron and tucked a strand of hair behind her ear before leaning over the hob to peer into the deep pan of gravy she was stirring.

"Smells good, Tony man!" I said twisting back round and grinning across.

He stood at the other end of the table, tousle haired, flashing one blade over the other as he sharpened the carving knife. The other three sat round, neat and tidy, chairs pulled up tight, waiting like hungry children. We were all on our best behaviour, and Falkland Island sheep-shagger jokes would not be part of the evening's entertainment. Tony took his eyes briefly off his task, grinned and nodded across at Ailsa's back. "I hope so chum." he said, "I'm bloody starving!"

I thought about it. They'd probably been working since early morning and were as hungry as us.

One of the lads had put the cans of lager he'd brought in his kit on the table. Ailsa moved them to one side clattering hot plates down in front of Tony. I couldn't see 'the look' but thought it might have said "manners". She went back to the range and picked up a thick cloth before stooping down to the heavy oven handles.

"Do you want a hand, love?" I said, making to get up.

She pushed the hair back again and hauled open the doors.

"No, you sit there," she said, and the heat from the oven hit me like a desert wind.

She brought the lamb, crackling and spitting, from the oven and, transferring it onto a big tin dish, where it hung generously over the edges, heaved it over to the table.

"There," she said smiling, looking round proudly at our mesmerised faces, "You'd better like lamb."

All eyes were on the dish. Brum had his knife and fork gripped firmly in each fist, ready on either side of his empty place mat.

"Won't be long love," she said, looking at him, and made her way back to the range.

The vegetables came over next and then the huge pot of gravy; Tony all the while carving and lifting great chunks of succulent lamb onto our waiting plates.

Our mission was to get the feel of the terrain, to drop in on the islanders, to make contact – friendly, if possible. It was called 'Hearts and Minds.'

A game? Maybe, but if it was, I tried to make it a sincere one. Show them you weren't just a bunch of trigger-happy grunts and that you didn't have two heads, that kind of thing. It occurred to me now though, that it worked both ways. If this had been a contest, then the Heathmans would have been six nil up before the end of the first half. But now, with our plates before us, and after our first taste of Falklands lamb, they would have won hands down.

After the scran that passed as food in the barracks, this simple roast, cooked just like your mums, was a mega 'blow out' fit for kings. Big Time!

Later that night, as we said our goodnights and made our way to our bunks, the warmth of whisky still in our mouths, I guessed that we had evened the score a little, our craic winning us back a few points. We'd had a good evening, sitting around the table till late. I'd seen a side to the islanders I hadn't experienced before, and one I liked. Tony and Ailsa were a hardworking young family, had fought their way up from being part of a shearing gang to owning this farm. They would tough it out for a way of life they clearly relished, and if it came to the crunch and you had to lay it on the line, you'd at least be fighting for someone you liked.

We left the following day, with Green Patch next on our agenda. This was a small settlement of farm buildings, wooden bungalows and the shearing shed where our two new friends had worked. It was one day's yomp to the north. We had a three-day stop here, and then headed back round the bases of Mount Vemet and Mount Longdon, over Wireless Ridge, and finally down the long slope to Moody Brook from the north.

Come Friday night, we were knackered, cleaned up, in civvies and in the noisy bar, listening to the craic about young Brasso and the two small pink arrivals which he had apparently bought and installed in a paddock behind one of the camp's sheds.

CHAPTER 6

ENTER THE PIGS

The camp's gym was really no more than a barn. To get there you had to cross the compound, past the parked up four tonners and circumnavigate the old derelict concrete shed known as Belsen. Like Moody Brook itself, the shed had a weird arrangement of flying buttresses holding up about fourteen compartments. Difference was, though, it was now a ruin. I'd passed it earlier, just after sun up, speculating as usual about the mystery surrounding the matelot who had been found many years back, hanging inside from one of the rafters. The derelict pile seemed to reek in the frozen air of death and decay. The gym stood a few yards behind and to one side.

I'd started my weights in earnest now and this morning's early start was no exception. The way I could see it, it was either keep fit or become an alcy. There was bugger all else to do. Earlier, the tin walls and plastic covered dojo mats had seemed to hold in a chill like a butcher's freezer – the fast wind blasting the outside seemed almost warm in comparison. An hour in though, and I was steaming, and the draft outside seemed like a good idea, so I draped a towel round my neck, opened the flimsy door and welcomed the icy blast. I'd pulled the towel up to wipe the beads of sweat from my face when Brasso, carrying a bundle in his arms, appeared just a few yards away, walking round the corner of Belsen as if he was making for the creek.

"Oi, Brasso lad," I shouted.

"'Kin 'ell, George." He jumped – I think he was a bit startled.

"Here, what's all this about two little piggies then?" I couldn't ask him in the bar the night before, because he didn't drink.

"They were all taking the piss last night man." I said rubbing my hair.

"Fuck them!" Belsen's tin roof rattled in the wind behind him. "They're a pair of right little beauties."

So it was true then. As he was speaking, another of the lads came round carrying a pile of gear. Brasso saw my expression and smiled.

"Before you ask, we're off down to the creek to put in some nets." he explained.

Shit, I thought. We'd had some nets in before and the only things we caught were soft nosed mullet and they tasted like crap.

"Well, if you catch any fish, Brasso lad, you can eat the buggers yourself."

I pulled a face.

"That's the beauty of my plan," he said, "no one else catches the buggers that come up the creek 'cos they taste like shit, but I reckon my pigs'll fuckin' love 'em!" He gave me a smug look. "You see? They'll eat anything. I'll be bloody quids in George, they'll fatten up in no time."

I watched him walk off down the slope. He was a cunning sod but you had to hand it to him. At least he had a plan. No wonder he was two-bob better off than Scrooge.

Throwing the towel over my shoulder, I went back into the shed to put away the weights.

CHAPTER 7

THE GLORY HOUR

Two months later the grunters had trebled in size. Slops from the galley and a steady diet of soft nosed mullet were working wonders, and, if you looked closely, you could see the pound signs flicking up like two slot machine symbols in Brasso's eyes every time he lovingly filled their trough. The pigs had given him something to do, and helped the time to pass.

As for me, I'd imposed a hard regime of fitness training on myself to counteract the boredom. Weight training in the gym and running, mostly along the coast road covering the six miles to town and back, or the half marathon which took me past the Beaver sea plane shed and across to Stanley Airport.

Visiting Port Stanley during my free time did little for me. There were just the three pubs, that is if you could call them that without breaking any trade description laws.

The truth is they resembled nothing like a pub (as we know it). Built out of timber, clad in weatherboard and painted just like the majority of the island's buildings, no matter what you did with them, whatever you called them, or colour you painted them, they still looked like little more than overgrown sheds.

The most popular with the lads was the "Globe Hotel" in the town centre. Set a couple of streets back from the quayside it was the place where everyone drank, from the governor down, and it was a favourite place for the island girls to clock the Marines. The others were 'The Rose' on the other side of town and a pub painted orange, run by an Argy. 'The Rose' was the opposite of a riot, and if you so much as swore within hearing distance of the landlord you were banned – for life!

So, on a weekend it was these three exciting night-spots, or our own mess that we'd christened 'The Ferkham Hall.' An apt name we thought, which just about summed up our mood. In fact, after several months on the islands it occurred to me that, if God had needed to give the world an enema, then the Falklands would have been a good place to start.

The last time I'd been in town was a good month after Brasso's pigs had arrived, and it was early on a freezing Sunday morning with the cloud layer down to ground level. The detachment rugby team were a man down and I'd been press-ganged into taking his place. It wasn't my game but I'd give it a go.

We had been playing for damn near ninety freezing minutes when I noticed the little gaggle of swearing supporters on the line getting slightly more animated, their faces blurring behind frozen breath of abuse. And it was as though I was the enemy. They were cheering on a huge islander who was bearing down on me, urging him on, like punters at a horse race.

Somehow the big guy had broken through our line, and he was closing in fast, steam coming in little short bursts from flared nostrils, big legs pounding, showering his pursuers with mud. The trouble was, he was making for the touch-line, and it was behind me.

When we collided it was like a steam train hitting a buffer, his giant frame folding around me like a sack of spuds. One of his knees pistoned up, catching me in the solar plexus knocking the wind from my body. Then a fist from one of his pursuers shot through, hammering the ball from his grasp, and I heard the breath leave his lungs as the pack hit us from behind, driving us deep into the liquid mud and gravel, sliding us over the line towards the feet of the disappointed groaning crowd.

Stars cleared, short painful bursts of breath began to fill my lungs again and the whistle sounded through the gusting wind as the ref trotted over. "Come along lads, not long to go now." He sounded anxious, half looking down at us, whistling again and pointing to 'the spot'. As he ran backwards he was looking at his watch and seemed to me to be making a calculation.

I hauled myself up, helping the big guy who was winded and being sworn at by the gaggle, out of the mud.

It had in fact been more like a war than a game, the sloping pock-marked pitch bearing a remarkable resemblance to a First World War battlefield. Twenty minutes before, I'd watched one of our team, Bob Fenson, being stretchered off with a broken leg, reducing the 'Defence Force' by one and upping the nasty retaliation tackles at the same time.

"Who needs enemies when you've friends like these bastards?" was running through my mind when I noticed the ref look at his wrist again, then blow his whistle twice, turn and abruptly walk towards the line.

It was like a film breaking down at the pictures. Both teams stopped as one. Faces looked up and across to the retreating black figure of the ref. Players picked themselves up from the mud where they had been fighting viciously for the ball, the steaming crowd walked muttering from the perimeter, disappearing into the fog, and it was all over.

Cold, wet and puzzled at the game's sudden end, I squelched across the windy field to our line, where I found Chubb and Hobbs loitering with the rest of the gathering team by the perimeter fence.

"OK, Chubby lad, where's the showers then?" I said, scraping some of the mud off my elbows and flicking it at him.

He looked at me, faking pity, "Piss off. We're off for a beer chum. No time for a bloody shower."

"What, like this?"

"You look lovely!"

As we spoke a driver pulled up at the gate, his vehicle pointing out of town, and the OC who had been part of the team pushed past us heading towards it.

"Here, Sir, aren't you coming for a pint with the lads Sir?" Chubby said in his best polite voice, as the boss came level.

"I'd love to Chubb, believe me," the OC said half turning in our direction, a streak of mud like war paint down his cheek. " 'Fraid I can't though. The governor's coming for lunch. Got to get back and cleaned up – probably why he rushed off so fast. Still maybe next time eh?"

"Sir."

I watched him push through the crowd, climb into the waiting Rover and head off towards the Barracks.

Hobbs was smiling ironically and Chubby had burst into his horrible low laugh as they watched him go.

"OK, you pair of bastards," I said, "so what should I know?"

Chubby turned and pointed over to the end of the field, still gurgling.

"Well?" I said.

"See the car?"

"Yes, what of it?" I looked more closely. It was the governor's red taxi that he was pointing at, and the ref was getting in the back. That was odd. As I watched, it pulled away heading towards Port Stanley. But it wasn't the only vehicle to be seen, as it pulled away our two Land Rovers turned up and parked, also facing towards town.

I looked back at Chubb and Hobbs. Smirks creased their faces.

"The Globe is the only pub on the island open on a Sunday," Chubby explained. "And seeing as how it only opens from 12 to 1, the governor, i.e. our friend the ref, being very thirsty after a hard game of rugby, is coming with us for a drink ain't he?"

He started to run towards the revving transport.

"Come on you silly sod. We've got one hour to get pissed!"

I looked at the clock on the dash as I crammed in to the first available seat. The Rover, stinking of sweat with its passengers covered in blood, snot and mud, bucked and leaned horribly, gaining speed as we left the field all four wheels spinning. It was still one minute to twelve and the pub was round the next corner.

Fuck the rugby. Rex Hunt had timed it perfectly. On the island, twelve to one on a Sunday was known as 'The Glory Hour'.

CHAPTER 8

A BRUSH WITH THE JUNTA

Late July found me up early – wearing civvies – and by 9 AM already in the air at twenty thousand feet.

I pushed back in my seat and unbuckled the belt. The Fokker F27 seats were narrow and in pairs and sergeant major Johnny Noone was jammed between me and the window.

Argentine Airline's corporate colours dominated the cabin. Blue plastic head covers on the square seat backs were lining the blue-carpeted central gangway. Overhead blue and white lockers crowded in at a forty-five degree angle to get maximum storage space into the claustrophobic tube of the fuselage. It was cramped, but I wasn't complaining. I just thanked my stars that I was off the island, and heading in the right direction.

On take off, the Rolls Royce Dart 6 Turbo Props had lifted us effortlessly from the short airstrip of Port Stanley. The Argentine Airlines pilot had hauled us round to starboard in a climbing arc and set our course to the north. I guessed that we were making cruising speed of no more than 250, although at our altitude the jet stream would determine our actual rate of knots.

Maybe the captain knew our ETA by now. But he didn't need to tell us, at least not yet. After all, it was still a long way to Buenos Aries, with a touch down first at Comodoro Rivadavia in the Golfo San Jorge, Patagonia. This passenger for one would be very happy to sit back and enjoy the flight.

The Sergeant Major had the 'diplomatic bag' resting on his knees, hand around the worn brown leather handle. He wouldn't let go of it until we got to the Embassy. I looked past him at the sky outside the window. We'd come through the murk.

The green cone of the prop and the blur of the blades were cutting between the white cloud layer which was at last below us and the impossibly blue heavens stretching towards a dazzling white horizon. Back on the ground it had been icy cold and grey for weeks and the colour outside the Perspex was like a tonic.

"Jesus! Look at that! Sunshine! Never thought I'd see it again!" I said loudly above the roar of the motors.

Johnny looked out through the perspex, and then back at me. "There'll be plenty more of that where we're going, old son" he half shouted back, then, patting the bag, pulled it up to his chest, closed his eyes, and leaned back in his seat. I followed his lead, enjoying the feeling of freedom, but keeping my eyes half open. After all I was riding shotgun on the diplomatic bag run, and it was my turn to play the 'heavy'.

Earlier that week, Hobbsie had reacted predictably when I wound him up, casually letting slip that I'd be away for a week in the sun.

"You lucky bastard, Tirptz!"

I'd scored a direct hit. "No luck in it, sunshine." I thought I'd emphasize the sun bit.

"Pure bloody skill son," I carried on. "Oh yeah, meant to ask. Got any sun-cream you can lend me?"

"Piss off!"

The 'diplomatic bag' run was once a month and we would take the duty in turns. Good thing was that the couriers had to be either an officer, or a senior NCO and one NCO. That's where I came in, so I figured there were some perks with the rank then, not just all responsibility.

Many weary hours later, we arrived, still in sunshine, in the land of Argentina.

The heat and the smell of Buenos Aires International hit me as I walked across the tarmac, and the bustle and clamour of the busy sophisticated airport, plus the sight of suited travellers and women in high heels was like a shot in the arm.

The diplomatic bag and our papers had a magic effect on the surly 'uniforms' loafing at the customs' gates, so much so that we were whisked through, almost politely, without the usual, time wasting macho posturing of the petty Latino officials.

Before we knew it, Johnny and I were outside the echoing halls, the ping-pong sound of the tannoy, followed by its pleasant female voice, floating over the hubbub behind us. Above, the airport's broad stainless steel canopy hung in the sky, keeping the smooth glass swing doors cool in the still hot sun. Car and coach horns and engine noise had taken over. Mercedes diesels were everywhere, drawing in and pulling out of the big tarmac semicircle, filling the place with their acrid fumes.

Johnny had done the run before so I followed him to the right of the main doors, pushing through the crowd to a quieter corner, and stood with him on the edge of the pavement. But I had no idea how we would find our transport.

"He'll find us," he said, in answer to my look.

Across the street, tall palms swayed above orange flowers in a formal garden, while the front of the high dun-coloured blocks behind, were cast in shade. A breeze had stirred the fronds. It started on the right-hand palm and I was watching it rippling down the line of trees when a car pulled in off the street, stopping a few feet away from us. It was a sandy coloured Mercedes of course – they all seemed to be the same colour – and it was wearing a taxi plate. The middle-aged driver got out, pulled off his shades, put them back in through the window onto the dash, and grinned.

"Embassy, Signor?"

"Yeah, that's us, pal."

"Si si." He hustled round to open the boot.

We walked across and piled in our cases. Then the driver went to take the leather bag from Johnny, to place it with the others.

"No." Johnny said shaking his head, "The bag stays with me, old son."

Later, in the cool lobby of the Embassy I couldn't get the grin off my face as I began to count again. Yes, two million pesetas! It was my spending-money for the week, and a great wedge of notes. Satisfied with my second count, I held it up to Johnny and kissed it.

"Christ, man, I've never been so rich. Who'd have thought it, me a bloody millionaire."

"It's not worth a lot," he said "I reckon it's about two hundred quid. Time you've paid your hotel bill you'll have about half left."

"That'll do," I said "I'll still be a pigging millionaire even then!" Then I had a thought. "Hey. Maybe I should take a picture. Brasso will be sick as a parrot." Still grinning I stuffed the notes in my pockets and followed Johnny down to the car.

The Airport taxi was a one-way trip, so 'the car' belonged to the Ambassador.

"Nice motor," I said, and I meant it, as the chauffer closed the heavy door with a clunk, before climbing into the driver's seat. But he made no reply, I guess he'd heard it all before. Instead, he ritualistically picked up his grey hat from the central console, placed it carefully over his immaculate comb-over hair, adjusted it in the rear view mirror, coughed as if about to make a speech, turned the key and pressed the little chrome button in the walnut dash.

We pulled away without a sound, leaving the dark shade of the underground garage for the bright sunshine of the main street. The tinted glass held back the glare and the air-conditioning kept the interior like a fridge. The big black limousine was the height of luxury and, as we pulled up at the hotel and a flunky came out for our bags, with two million pesetas busting a hole in my pocket, and a week off; suddenly, the Falkland Islands seemed a long, long way away.

We left the hotel early the next morning, the heavy glass doors swishing shut behind us, as we stepped out into the sunshine.

A slight breeze was playing with the triangular flags on the smart bureau opposite; it was picking them up, before brushing them against the bronze-slatted wall behind. Above them, tall neon letters encased in a steel oblong box climbed the building, the glass advertisement pale and dull in the bright early sun.

Next door, a glass-domed portico stuck out, with stylised balconies rising from the same marble facade, one, two, three, four high, and festooned with vivid flowers. Over these, elegant stonework jettied, supporting the huge cornices of the roof, affording the balconies cool shade in the equinox hours.

Between us and the heavens, wires supporting streetlights, looking like huge glass upside-down bowler hats, criss-crossed the street, covering the short distance from building to building. In perfect symmetry they cut like a draughtsman's lines, central to the street and arrow-true, towards the high trees in the park at a far junction. Whilst below, a profusion of illuminated box signs ascended the walls or hung out diagonally as if suspended in the South American air. They announced the shops and galleries underneath, punctuated the sky above and peeped through the circular arch of a great clock, hanging fifty yards down the street, below its frame of tubular steel.

The gentle wind felt warm as we walked amongst the well dressed early shoppers. It swirled around in little eddies, clearing away the night chill, filling the air with the heady scent of hibiscus-filled tubs that appeared to run the entire length of the street.

Our route would take us in the direction of the park and the city-centre. It seemed to be the general flow of the foot traffic anyway. People were dressed in heavy coats and one kiddie was wearing an anorak with its hood up. Ahead of me, a tall woman in tight white trousers and a short fur coat walked arm in arm with her partner. He pulled up his collar as I watched.

To me it was like a breezy summers day on the Sunderland coast and yet to these people, used to the intense heat of their climate, this was the coldest month of the year. Temperatures would still only drop to around fifty … Fahrenheit!

We had decided to play the tourist and visit the sights: Cleopatra's Needle, the Pink Palace and a graveyard. The last destination was suggested last night over supper in Jock the Embassy caretaker's flat.

Jock was a former soldier. He knew the town well and would look after us while we were here. His Ghanaian wife had cooked us a slap-up meal in friendship and appreciation for the ritual bottle of duty free.

"Hey, I know where you should go while you're here," she said, listening to Jock giving us directions, whilst clearing away the dishes.

We looked up.

"Evita's Tomb," she said decisively, then smiled broadly. "Have you seen the musical?"

Well now, would we?

"No love," Johnny said, as she walked back to the kitchen.

I didn't answer. I just looked at Jock and grinned. The West End was a long way from the muddy ditches and dark alleys of Northern Ireland, where we had been stationed the year before.

"Well even so, you should go and have a look at her tomb anyway! She was a good woman, a Saint!" she shouted through from her kitchen. "And you can tell your friends you've seen it."

So Jock had dutifully given us directions, and we had decided to pay a visit.

We reached the park crossing the busy ring road, where the traffic noise was intense after the calm of the pedestrian zone. Here a flock of pigeons, startled by the child wearing the anorak, left the grass and wheeled round into the blue sky, their wings slapping like distant gunshots.

Our route took us into the hub of the city. Important looking buildings lined the wide plazas, separated from the traffic by broad borders filled with trees and palms. The pavements were wide and teaming with humanity. Ahead a crowd had formed outside some kind of church. At least, I guessed that's what it was by a statue of the bearded Christ being carried shoulder high on a platform.

The gaudily painted effigy was moving between two of the giant stone pillars that held up the great roof. Someone had attached speakers to two of the pillars, and above the heads on the other side of the crowd an old van was parked with four big bell speakers mounted on its roof. The last time I'd seen one was in Belfast during an election. And there was a lot of noise. A woman's angry voice was shouting from the middle of the crowd, somewhere near the effigy Jesus. Men and lots of women, young and old, with drawn faces looked on, craning their necks with expressions of distaste and exasperation. This wasn't a happy gathering. No-one was smiling.

Intrigued by what was going down, I brought my camera up quickly to get a shot. As I depressed the button, two men were looking directly back from the crowd, their expressions a mix of suspicion and fear.

Not wishing to see any more, or understanding what was going on, we moved on quickly. It was the first ugly side I'd seen to this seemingly wealthy and civilised city.

Once on the other side of the crowd we crossed a narrow side street before continuing our journey once again along the broad pavement. The strident voice in the crowd behind us could still be heard, but receded with every step, getting weaker beneath the roar of the passing traffic before finally dying, becoming indistinguishable, snubbed out by the indifferent noise of the metropolis.

Walking on in silence, I got to thinking about what I may have just witnessed. It reminded me that we were not sight-seeing in a free city. Far from it. The sun may have been shining and the pavement cafés busy but if reports were true, then this was the capital of the most violent and ruthless military dictatorship in Latin America.

I shoved my hands in my pockets and looked down at the pavement, my head still full of the words the woman had been shouting, "Donde estan? Donde estan?" Hadn't I heard the cry before? It stuck in my mind. I focussed hard on the words.

"Donde estan?" "Donde estan?" Then I remembered.

I'd seen a TV news report back home, God knows how it had got out of the country. It was about Argentina's 'disappeared ones', the 'desaparecidos'. In the film, a group of women, calling themselves 'The Mothers of the Plaza De Mayo', were defying the president's ban on free speech, standing arm in arm outside a big building, shouting "Donde estan?" over and over in defiance.

It translated as "Where are they? Where are they?"

Since this present Junta seized power, tens of thousands of people had literally disappeared. Anyone they thought was a threat was removed. With a ruthless efficiency they had started with what they called 'suspected terrorists', and quickly spread their net to include unionists, students, teachers, housewives, non-conformist members of their own party and security forces, journalists and academics. The list went on and on: actors, nuns, priests, friends of any one they considered to be subversive, friends of friends, children and even newborn babies. In fact, if the report was true, the Junta couldn't sink much lower.

A scooter sped past, its crackling exhaust breaking in on my thoughts. It was a grim reflection but, if the people outside the church were making some kind of a protest, then I was probably not the only one watching with interest. In which case, by the time I processed the photograph, some of the faces looking back at me would be lucky if they had seen another days sunrise.

After another ten minutes walking, with the street cafes having petered out, something across the road caught my attention, pulling me up fast.

"Hang on a sec, Johnny," I said, unzipping the fabric lid of the camera case. Opposite us, a line of tall dark trees interspersed with palms stopped, leaving a clear view, before starting again a few hundred feet on.

"Bloody hell, see what you mean George," Johnny said, following my line of vision.

Behind the gap in the planting, set close to the road, stood a broad building maybe twenty stories high. Square windows, set into the stone façade, faced the street in perfect symmetry around the business-like central doors. Outside, at the entrance from the road, stood a sign giving the impression it was some kind of admiralty building. At least that's how I interpreted it but what interested me was the roof or rather what was on it. Above the mansards a tangle of aerials and antennae grew like a forest of steel in a kind of paranoid profusion. I'd never seen so much hardware on the roof of a building before, and automatically pointed the Olympus.

As I took aim a sharp shout, "Hey senor!", came angrily from one of two men that appeared on my right, the direction from which we had come. Something jarred about their unexpected appearance. There was hardly anyone about on this stretch of the broad pavement, and it seemed strange that I hadn't noticed them before.

I triggered the camera. "Zip, zip." The shutter closed twice, capturing the images I wanted. Then I turned my head to look at the man that had called out. He had stopped about four yards away, keeping his distance. Stocky, dark haired, wearing a blue padded jacket, he was wagging his finger at me.

"No Photografee-a senor!" he said angrily, then animatedly started pointing at the camera with one hand, while holding out the other hand, palm up, beckoning with his fingers.

"No Photo!" he repeated. "You! Si you, give camera. Pronto!"

Johnny walked back the few paces to join me while I tucked the camera back into its case.

"I get the impression he doesn't think you should have done that George," he said quietly, "and something tells me he wants your camera." He paused, watching the man who was again repeating his demand, then looked up at me ironically.

"Well, aren't you going to give it him? He's asking so nicely."

I scratched my head and grinned back. "Yeah, right, maybe I should have it gift wrapped."

While we were talking, the other man, the ugly one, who had been stood by one of the trees, came closer and made a snatch towards the camera. He was quick, but I sidestepped, cuffed his arm down with the heel of my palm and shoved him away by his shoulder.

I dropped the grin now, narrowing my eyes as he swung back round towards me rubbing his forearm.

"Wrong move sunshine," I said softly, staring into his little black eyes. I had no idea if he could understand me, but hoped he'd get the message. The last thing we wanted was a fight. But I could see that he was going to come on again, so I backed a step and lowered my stance.

"Whoa, whoa!" Johnny stepped between us, hands up at shoulder height, facing the two men.

"Tourists," he said, smiling, looking from one to the other. Then he hissed "keep it cool George," through the side of his mouth. "We're just tourists my friends. Holiday photos, that's all."

By now, a few passers by had stopped and were watching us and the two men, suspiciously.

"Holiday?" The first man looked at the other and they talked quickly together. "Holiday, is vacation?" he said to Johnny, doing his best to look shrewd.

"Si." A voice from the small crowd, looking on, spoke out. "Si, vacation." The first man looked at the owner of the voice then back at us.

"So Tooreesta, you Tooreesta?" He said slowly, revealing crooked teeth in what I took to be an attempt at a smile.

"That's us pal," Johnny replied. "Tooreesta."

"OK." The first man waved a dismissive hand. "You go."

The crowd began to disperse at his words, avoiding our eyes as we backed off a few paces before turning. Ugly was playing the hard-man and watching me all the way.

"I think he fancies me," I said.

"Probably George, he's ugly enough. But never mind him, what the bloody hell was that all about?"

"Christ knows." I patted the camera case. "Sensitive bastards aren't they?"

We walked on a few paces and when I turned round they were gone.

Years later, I learned that there were more than three hundred secret detention centres in Argentina used for indescribable acts of barbarity, depravation and torture. One of them, the most notorious; masquerading as The Naval Mechanics School (Escuela Mechanica de la Armada) was on the Avenida Libertador in the centre of Buenos Aires – our route that day.

CHAPTER 9

THE RICH AND THE DEAD

An hour later I folded the city guide and slid it into my back pocket. There was no need for it now, the cemetery had finally come into sight. We had reached the leafy district of La Recoleta.

We had been following trees spasmodically since leaving the hotel, their cool shade cast from dark boughs, fluttering high above the sidewalks throughout the main streets of the city, like giant fans in the breeze. Here they grew in even greater abundance, their trunks sending criss-cross shadows, like the stripes of a zebra, across the pavements as we walked.

It was obvious that the city was rich and, by the look of it, there was probably nowhere wealthier than this stylish neighbourhood. The grand buildings here had somehow taken on a kind of self-important smugness, getting even more up their own arses the closer they got to the cemetery. The whole place reeked of wealth. It was as though the moneyed classes wanted to be as close to their final resting-place as they could get.

Covering the distance between the dappled trunks we passed from shadow to sunlight and then back again into the shade, closing in now on the entrance.

Across the street, a villa caught the light in dull reflection from its sombre gray lead guttering. The studded door, heavy and forbidding, was shut tight against the world. In many ways it resembled the big houses that crowded around the municipal cemetery back home, different styles, worlds apart but still the windows carried that same dead look, as though nothing lived behind them, like eye sockets in a skull.

On reaching the entrance gates, I could see why it was included on the tourist 'must see' list in the city guide. Jock's missus had told us a bit about the place last night but you had to see it to believe it.

"Jesus Christ! Grand or what?" I said, squinting against the sun at the columns that rose majestically on either side of us. High above our heads they were supporting an ornately carved canopy, like something from an epic Biblical film set. I guess St Peter was in the architect's mind when he sat down to draw this one and it was no accident that the stone used was pearly white. It made an impressive entrance but we were still unprepared for what waited for us on the other side.

Johnny stepped through and I followed, hearing him whistle softly through his teeth.

"Wow! Do 'emselves proud don't they?" he said almost in a whisper.

And at first glance I had to agree.

It was as though we'd left one city, the real one where scale and perspective made sense, and had entered a kind of alien city in miniature.

A broad walkway stretched away before us, dead straight, mimicking the streets outside, but paved in a kind of semi-glazed tile, each one fluted and set at an angle to the next. Trees again lined the route but this time each one a specimen – the kind you find in grand parks. Pines with wispy fragrant branches, and monkey-puzzles, standing like primeval reminders amongst the others.

Between the trees, blocks, shapes and plinths of carved stone stood like pieces on a chess board, some mounted by angels or deeply hooded figures in bronze and marble, eyes cast down in sanctity and mourning. From others, proud horses carried ramrod straight old men. The one nearest me was streaked in verdigris, the pale green dust etching deep into the lines of his fierce old face. It filled the crevices of his moustache and circled the medals on his chest as he readied his steed for battle.

From this central avenue flowed a series of side streets and lanes splitting up the whole. They formed the city blocks, one after the other as far as I could see before becoming blurred by the verdant trunks and confusing shadows.

A group of people ahead of us, one wearing a black gaucho hat, left the drag and filed down one of the turnings. The children were carrying flowers and the man in the hat was toting some kind of plaque about the size of a dinner tray. As they disappeared, I noticed a movement on my left. A grey cat had appeared from behind one of the plinths. It walked lazily, tail up, from the dusty flowerbed that framed the base, into dappled shade and then into the full sun as it crossed our path, then disappeared as quietly as it had materialized, amongst the statues on the other side. It did not give us a second glance.

I remembered the night before and the verbal instructions that had been given to us.

"Don't bother looking for the Peron tomb either," Jock's wife had said, " 'cos you won't find her there. You need Duarte, remember that. Duarte – her family name. That's where she is, God rest her soul." And she had made the sign of the cross.

I'd made a kind of sketchy map to her instructions, but I'd only been half listening, not realizing the scale of the place. Looking around now, and then down at the scribble on the margin of the city guide, it was obvious that it was next to useless. Johnny had been looking at the sketch as well.

"Oh well, come on then George." he said, scratching his head after turning the page this way and that. "We've got this far, so we might as well give it a go."

We knew she wasn't on this main drag, that much I remembered, so we took the first lane to our right. It was like a miniature of the central avenue, without the trees or statues, as there just wasn't room, but I got the feeling they'd have put them in if they could.

The similarity was in the crazy little buildings that now rose on either side of us, not set back like those in the main street, but just as bizarre; diminutive temples and tiny chapels crowned with all manner of classical gables and scaled-down domes. From some, rose stone crosses and from others angels but not like those on the deck in amongst the trees. These soared above, wings open, frozen in flight.

These were the homes of the dead – the rich and the dead.

They lined the lane, crowding in, bright on one side with the warm sun and cast into gloom on the other, each one not much bigger than a single garage. Like so many Council Estate lock-ups, gone mad.

We read the plaques as we walked on. One thing we knew for certain was that Eva Peron's mausoleum was made out of dark marble, maybe black, so anything too light we left out.

Some were more fancy than others, so much so that, regardless of the colour, it was impossible not to stop and look like some kind of mawkish sightseer.

Passing from one to the other, it soon became apparent that, although the façade of each tomb appeared to be made from a different stone or marble and of a different design to its neighbours, making an odd mishmash of a terrace, they all had the same characteristic: an entrance door, usually dead centre, and plaques with names, fixed either side and over the lintel.

Many of the doors were solid but others you could see through as they were glass panelled from top to bottom – these doors were set behind fancy wrought iron outer shutters.

I looked through the first one I found to see an image which turned out to be repeated in a similar vein, over and over, throughout the vast cemetery.

Johnny joined me, holding his hand against the ironwork to shield off the light.

"It's like a little church," he said, pushing his face closer to the glass.

"Aye, it's fantastic. It's their own little chapel. Look at that will you. Someone's been in. There's even fresh flowers in the vase."

We didn't speak loudly but in a kind of hushed reverence. I don't know why, but it never occurred to me that people, living people, went inside these places. I thought tombs were locked up tight and only opened when needed. It was only later that I noticed the polished well-used look on many of the handles.

Inside, this one was painted white like a Franciscan Cell, the floor bare, apart from an altar on the back wall, draped with a velvet cloth. The flowers stood in the centre behind a polished brass crucifix flanked by two candlesticks. Clear water nearly filled the vase, and two petals rested where they had fallen, at the base of the cross.

There were pictures on the walls as well. Not many, maybe three or four to a wall. I noticed two on my left were paintings but most seemed to be photographs, black and whites, no colour. On the inner rear wall a smiling child looked back at me.

It made me think of back home and visiting elderly relatives as a kid, where the dead of the two great wars hung on the walls of the front parlours. These were the rooms of the widows and mothers who were still grieving – rooms that you peeped into as a child at Christmas, rooms where nobody laughed.

I pulled away from the glass, feeling a shudder of cold as though a cloud had momentarily covered the sun and stepped back into the centre of the lane. There, it was as warm as ever. I squinted up. Not a cloud in the sky, just the one lone gull high up, wheeling in from the south. I let it pass and moved on.

Not all the residents were so well looked out for. I came across one tomb where the glass was smashed behind the bars and had obviously been so for years. The place was full of litter and stank of cats. Strangely, it was one of the bigger places and had once had a magnificent dome, the shaped rafters of which were now stripped bare, standing silhouetted against the sky. Amazingly, despite the squalor of the burial chamber and the dereliction of the roof, its huge angel still flew, wings-outstretched, from the very pinnacle, looking as clean and bright as the day it left the sculptor's chisel.

Another, a few blocks on, stunk for other reasons. It was clean enough, just full of brooms and other gear with the janitor's bucket taking pride of place on the altar. As we passed, the unmistakeable tang of Jeyes Fluid, or its Latin equivalent, drifted strongly through the still air.

I guess it was for the cats. The place seemed to be infested with them and I could see one now at the end of the lane, its black and white fur picking up the sun as it emerged from the shadow of a cross.

Many of the mausoleums had flowers left outside on the tilted walkway. One had so many that they were piled up in front, so deep they came part way up the door, spilling over, nearly filling the passage. A mouldering bronze bust stood outside another, just left there haphazardly. It watched me wistfully as I passed. For some reason the poor old sod appeared to have been evicted.

Finally, after two hours, we found what we had come for, the Duarte tomb. At first glance it was unremarkable, in many ways similar to all the rest, no bigger or smaller and certainly no more grand.

But there was something about the simplicity of the place that made the search worthwhile. Amongst all the surrounding cloy of pompous piety, this place had a gentle clean line that said more about elegance and the former beauty of its occupant than all the twiddly bits in the world could do for its neighbours.

The naivety of the way it was dressed made the difference complete.

Chains of wild flowers were hung on the fancy iron-work and single flower heads were poked in all around the big brass cross that filled the centre of the door. It was as though the crucifix was shielding the entrance to the tomb – floating in a field of vivid colour. On the floor outside was a single bloom still wrapped in cellophane.

We didn't go up to the mausoleum directly but hung back a little and waited. A woman in a bright shawl was standing in front, close to one of the flat pillars. It was she who had laid the flower on our approach. She was making no sound but her lips moved in the reflection of the polished stone.

As far as I knew then, Eva Peron had lain at La Recoleta since her death. I've since learned different. The facts, as usual, being far stranger than fiction. Even after her death her corpse still had a macabre role to play in the politics of Argentina, having a direct bearing on the events that would finally lead me to the frozen islands of the South Atlantic.

The Argentines, many of whom even now are still much in love with Eva Peron, have so muddled fact with fiction over the years that it's difficult to extract the truth from the legend. Rumours and stories have become blurred with time and corrupted by the peoples' determination to hang on to the good myths and forget the unsavoury. You can't blame them, as for a brief time, Eva Peron brought them hope and gave the poor a voice. Up to her short period of kindness and in the decades after her death, indeed right up to Argentina's invasion of the Falklands, the country's history makes for violent and bloody reading.

One thing, however, is undeniable and certain, Eva's 'rags to riches' story is a classic, a fairytale come true.

'Beautiful young peasant girl leaves home to seek fame and fortune in the big city'. Many would have dreamed of it, but Eva did it. Stardom as a radio actress in her own show brought her an introduction into society and courtship from handsome soon-to-be-president Juan Peron. Marriage, followed by her elevation, when Peron gained power in 1946, to Argentina's unassailable First Lady.

This was pretty breathtaking, even by fairytale standards, so you'd think that that would do. But not Eva Peron – she had her own agenda and her own mission.

Once in a position of authority, Eva's influence brought about huge unheard-of changes in Argentina's social conditions, especially for the poor, 'the Descamisado's' (the shirtless ones).

This was her dream – she would not forget them, nor forsake them.

In the poor she saw herself. She had been raised as one of five illegitimate children in a poor village. She spoke their language and knew their needs. She enveloped them with her love, and maintained her faith until her untimely death.

They, the shirtless ones, saw her quite literally as their living saint and it was only they that she allowed to use her peasant name Evita. To all else, especially the rich that she despised, she was Eva Peron, First Lady.

Before her agonising death at the age of thirty-three from uterine cancer, Eva had established her Social Aid Foundation, which created hundreds of schools, dozens of hospitals with trained nurses to run them and dispensed money to the poor and needy.

Through her Peronist Feminist party she furthered the rights of Women. She was so determined to bring about change that she would even deal with hardships one at a time if necessary, taking urchins from the street into the presidential palace to bathe and feed them and treat their injuries and scabies. Her work rate was phenomenal.

What's difficult to reconcile, though, is the fact that, alongside her undeniably great contribution to the poor, she was supposedly some kind of crypto fascist and her acceptance of the lifestyle she enjoyed with her husband, the President. It's inconceivable that she didn't know about his brutal policies, his repression of freedom of speech and his imprisonment of dissidents.

But did she agree?

During Peron's rule with Eva by his side, Argentina became a haven for the world's most evil butchers of the human race. Thousands of murderers, their hands soaked with the blood of innocents, found their way to Peron's embrace.

Nazi war criminals Adolf Eichman, 'The Angel Of Death' Mengele, and the Croatian Fascist Dictator Ante Pavelic were among the maggots that found their way to Argentina's shores.

The psychopath Pavelic was personally responsible for the torture and genocide of one third of Croatia's Serbs. His 'Ustase' followers' acts of utmost savagery and cruelty so horrified the Nazis that even they acted to halt the butchery, arresting one of his most notorious commanders and disarming his detachment.

When Pavelic arrived in Argentina, thousands of his Ustase sadists would soon join him. They walked free in the streets and rubbed shoulders in the bars and restaurants with the people of Buenos Aires. It was incredible. The henchmen would be just fine. Juan Peron had a new security advisor – their boss Ante Pavelic.

Little wonder that Che Guevara was amongst Peron's dissidents.

It was against this backdrop that Eva's soul left her body. She was just thirty-three years old and the year was 1952.

In three years Juan Peron was deposed by the military. When he left so did Eva's body but they did not go together. Eva's beautifully embalmed corpse had become an icon since her death, synonymous with the nation's once great hope of social justice. When Juan fled the country into exile, Eva's body simply disappeared.

The oligarchy had spirited it away as it had become far too dangerous. Even after her death Evita's cadaver was seen as a threat. The rich had hated her as much as she had despised them. Yes, the new Military junta would see to it that her people, 'The Shirtless Ones', were kept firmly in their place.

The body gave them problems. It exerted its own strange power over them. Their obsession with death and superstition made them afraid to destroy it and even more afraid to bury it in Argentina lest the tomb become found and used as a rallying point for a Peronist revival.

So they moved it about. Evita's remains were 'on the road' for sixteen years.

Tales have it that they rested awhile in Germany, were interred in Italy under another name and even at one time hidden in an anonymous piece of wooden furniture in a military office back in Argentina. Perhaps we will never know the truth. It wasn't until 1971 that Peron, living with his new wife Isabel in Madrid, was finally given the body back. The junta were decidedly rocky and the reuniting was no more than a cynical peace gesture.

At this point the stories take on an even more macabre twist.

Isabel wanted the mystical power that she believed exuded from the corpse and, in an attempt to absorb Evita's persona, would lie on top of the coffin or even, as some stories tell, would lie in it, next to the rotting cadaver.

Maybe it worked. Two years after the body became hers to use, her dreams of becoming the new Evita appeared to be coming true. Her husband had once again seized power, flying home in 1973 from exile to riots that saw the death of four hundred people. Juan Peron was once again the President of Argentina and, with a stunning stroke of arrogance, he made Isabel his Vice President.

On his death the following year, she succeeded him. It was breathtaking. Isabel was now in a position of even greater power than his last wife, the champion of the Descamisados.

Peron had left Eva's body in Spain when he returned to Argentina but Isabel, now that she ruled, ordered that it be flown home where she had it laid in state next to her late husband. At last the corpse was once more in its homeland.

There's no telling whether Evita could have changed Argentina's future had she lived but what now took place, after Peron's death, is a matter of fact.

The charity and the goodness that had once lived within Evita's corpse could not be transferred to another after her death, instead only evil and suffering were unleashed.

The woman who had so wanted Evita's power had, by a wicked turn of events, gained it, and now that she possessed it, she was determined to used it.

She used the power against her own people: the people that demonstrated in the streets outside her palace for freedom and social justice, the people who remembered the promise and the kindness that their living saint had once held out to them; 'the Descamisados' that had once nearly tasted justice – Evita's followers.

Isabel gave the order for the military to 'annihilate' subversion and terrorism and, by so doing, she plunged Argentina into many years of turmoil, torture camps and mass murder. She had let loose the forces of cruelty and darkness. The cancer had spread and the evil had flourished.

By the time the evil had run its course, at least thirty thousand men, women, children and babies had been 'disappeared.'

Looking at the tomb that day, as it basked in the warm sunshine of the peaceful cemetery, there was not a hint of the bizarre journey taken after death by the troubled remains within. To us it was just a place of rest, with an old woman at its door, who, after having carefully laid down a flower, stood quietly by one of the pillars, moving her lips and fiddling with some beads.

We waited patiently until she had finished her silent conversation, crossed herself, tidied her headscarf in the mirror of the polished stone and turned to leave. But she did not go straight away, Seeing us, she stopped and began talking rapidly in her own tongue, gesturing at the flowers with old hooked fingers.

"Si, si, aye, very nice luv," I said. I had no idea what she was saying but it seemed to please her. So we walked across to her nodding, and gesticulating that we did not understand. I could see her expression changing to kindliness as she registered that we were foreigners.

We stopped outside the tomb and she eyed us shrewdly, as though we were children at a special treat, then began speaking again, but this time very slowly and deliberately. Whatever she said sounded kind and proud, most of it meaning absolutely nothing to us, only the words 'Sancta' and 'Evita' coming through loud and clear.

When she left, I stepped up to the door, the scent of the decoration strong as I held my face close to the glass. There was just room to see between the foliage which dappled the interior. Inside there was no grandeur – it was flowerless and almost bare. What little light that seeped through, glinted off a crucifix mounted on a table. Behind it, as my eyes gradually got used to the gloom, I picked out the end of a coffin. It was just visible, dissected by a confusion of shadows that dappled the back wall. Heavier geometric bars of dark light also lay across the casket adding to the camouflage. The darkest was shed from the ornament on the little table, it was the shadow of the Cross, the dark side of the little polished Holy Cross.

CHAPTER 10

GUNS IN DOORWAYS

Two nights later, my desert-wellies making little squeaking noises on the shiny slabs of the broad city centre pavement, I made my way back to the hotel. It was late, but there were still plenty of people about, at least around the pavement cafés that transformed at night into the city's bars. I looked around as I walked. It was weird. There was something about the place, something in the air. The whole atmosphere felt wrong, kind of false.

Despite the lively nightlife, the music coming from clubs, and the amount of cheap booze available, the people behaved with a kind of courteous restraint. Groups sat chatting and laughing politely around cloth-covered tables with waiters weaving between them toting small glasses on trays. Taxis came and went, dropping off and picking up, people strolled along the broad, well-lit pavements whilst lovers sat tête-a-tête or walked arm in arm between the planters. All very nice, but difficult to get my head round. I mean, Jesus, it was Friday night for Christ's sake, this was no way to behave. If the lads had been with me, we'd have been chucking the seats around by now at the very least.

The restraint was unnatural. *— NOT SO TO BE DRUNK IN THE CITY IS SEEN AS DISGRACE*

I crossed another junction and turned off from the main street into a pedestrian zone away from the traffic noise. The upside-down bowler-hat streetlights swayed gently above in the breeze, casting a dimmer light than the lamp posts on the main drag, and the café and bars were further apart between the dim shop doorways. In fact, it became much darker in patches so you kind of walked from one bright spot to another.

It was in one of these murky patches that I became acquainted with the real Buenos Aires. The reason for the restraint and good behaviour was suddenly to become very obvious. *—NOT THE CUSTOM TO GET DRUNK ✱*

Smoke first drew my attention to him.

A little way ahead of me, on my side of a planter, a little cloud of strong tobacco had trickled from one of the recessed doorways. I don't smoke but it was unmistakeably Turkish. Whatever the brand, it slowed me down and put me on my toes. You don't hang around in dark doorways for nothing. Silently, I moved level with the opening, turning my head to look in, reasoning that if some bastard jumped me I'd at least see him coming.

He was as surprised as I was. Fag between his fingers, he was taking another

✱A LOT OF THESE PEOPLE WOULD HAVE ITALIAN ORIGINS — USED TO CAFE SOCIETY

drag as I came level. It was the ugly man I had brushed with on the way to the cemetery. He coughed as he dropped the telltale smoke in a shower of sparks, and his hand flew to the trigger of a gun.

Pump action shotguns are bad news at the best of times, but he was twitchy and looked to me to be decidedly trigger-happy. Bad combination.

Plus, he was not alone. There was another guy on his right, tucked tight in to the recess, his face showing irritation that I had seen them.

They were dressed like cops. 'Ugly' wore a black jumper with epaulets but the other guy, wearing a cap covered in braid, and a leather coat, would have been more at home in a Nazi war movie. Also, I could see that he was really pissed off. The way he waved his rifle at my stomach being the give away sign. His face was livid in the half light, partly with me I guess for staring in, but probably more for the stupid git that had just lit up.

"Vamoose! Rapido!" He hissed, waving the barrel dangerously.

I didn't need a second warning, the rifle strap was hanging low by his knees – a real amateur – and, like Ugly, he was also twitchy as hell. So working on the principal that sweaty and nervous trigger fingers have been known to start the shit flying, I was out of there fast.

There were more guys further down, and more still on the road to the hotel. Reaching it, grabbing my key and turning in for the night, I mused over what I'd seen.

It was classic: there were probably guns in doorways throughout the city but they wouldn't be interested in me as I'd soon be gone. No. They'd be watching the locals.

The message to the good people of Buenos Aires was chillingly clear. Step out of line, laugh at the wrong joke, and you wake up in the morgue.

CHAPTER 11

A REVEALING FLIGHT

I wasn't sad to leave Latin America. In fact, I was almost glad to be flying back to the islands. You knew where you were there – boring yes, but free, something I was used to.

After a week in the capital I'd started to notice things. The guns in doorways at night were obvious but a heavy presence of military vehicles and police-cars on the streets during the day and cops toting sub-machine guns also had a numbing affect. You'd have a job to turn a blind eye to the kind of oppression that seemed to stalk the streets. It was obvious that things were building and, if anything, the tension seemed to have increased in the last few days before we left.

That morning, I frowned past Johnny at the turbulent sky framed in the thick Perspex window of the passenger jet.

"Getting shitty out there now George!" He shouted above the roar of the engines.

"Tell me about it." The dark clouds, sporadic just a few minutes ago, were filling the horizon. "Bet you can't wait to get back."

"Don't you worry about me, old son," he patted the diplomatic bag, "another month and its back to the hotel."

"Jammy sod."

"No jam in it." He leant back, closed his eyes and tapped his upper arm with two fingers. "You have to earn it, George. Get yourself a couple more of these. They make all the difference."

Taking his lead, I stretched out my legs and thought about my options. I'd read my magazine from front to back and then flipped back through it the other way. That was out so it was either sleep, study the flight deck cabin door a few rows ahead or carry on looking at the clouds. Great.

I eased my shoulders, letting my head find the cushion, and listened to the two Spanish women in the seats behind. One gave a short cackling laugh while the other carried on rabbiting. Like the jets propelling us, they hadn't given it a rest since take off.

The fact that the weather had altered was no big surprise – it does when you're heading towards the world's southern pole. Inevitably it had been worsening by the mile since leaving Buenos Aires. The sky was brightest blue as we gained height, with not a cloud to be seen. Then a white haziness, wispy at first, built up to huge cumulus, as we put down for our fuel-stop at Comodoro Rivadavia.

Half dozing, I watched a woman, who had been sat with two squabbling kids three or four rows down, get up, steady herself on the seat back, and head past me towards the rear.

We'd been hugging the South American coast for hours but, now that we were crossing deeper waters, the South Atlantic's Antarctic weather stream was hitting us full on.

There was no blue to be seen, just different shades of grey. You could almost see the cold that would greet us. Port Stanley would be shrouded in a winter of ten below if we were lucky. I shuddered and looked up to where my bag was stowed, glad that I'd packed my Tog Jacket just under the zip. I pulled back my sleeve and scanned my watch. Another hour to touchdown.

The woman came back, brushed past me and sat back down with her kids.

Johnny hadn't moved and the diplomatic bag on his knees wasn't likely to go anywhere so maybe it was a good idea to get in thirty minutes myself. My eyes swept the cabin. Half the fifty odd passengers I guessed were asleep like Johnny and in thirty seconds I would join them.

It was probably the slight turbulence that brought me back round, my watch checking in that I'd done most of the thirty. The plane was doing tricks, thumping on hard pockets of air as we lost height. I yawned and swallowed to unblock my ears.

Johnny's head nodded to the side as he snorted awake. The frozen air straight off the 'continent of ice' not far away would be lying in layers over little pockets of warmth, feebly rising from below. There would still be a temperature difference coming off the land as the final bit of summer heat drained away. I couldn't think why it bothered, the ice always won.

"We must be nearly home!" I shouted. "Wonder how fat Brasso's porkers have got?"

"God knows. The rate they were putting it on they could have doubled their size in the past week." Johnny grinned rubbing his eyes.

We thumped down another hole and began our bank to starboard. I'd watched flights coming in whilst on armed duty at the airfield so I knew where we were. Confirming my reckoning, the cloud lifted a tad, revealing the bay and our height through the murk outside the starboard windows.

This was the easy bit. We were crawling now, ready for the final approach. Soon we'd be swinging round to begin the only way down onto the airstrip, a precise operation – difficult and over the rocks.

Behind me was a movement. The steward had emerged from the rear galley and, for some reason, had taken this chance to make his way down the aisle to the flight deck. I dragged my leg in to let him pass.

"Gracias, senior."

"No problem, pal."

He entered the cabin, pulling the door shut behind him, but it didn't catch. Great, I should be close enough to the cabin to see our touchdown, or at least that's what I hoped. Slowly, with the vibration of the motors, the door opened a few inches. On our final turn, the angle of the plane dipped on the side of the hinges and the door swung open, revealing the inside of the flight deck.

I nudged Johnny and inclined my head towards the front.

"Get a load of that."

The flight deck was full, literally standing room only. It was packed with 'uniforms'. Apart from the pilot and co-pilot, there were probably another five, some of them high ranking, their caps covered in scrambled egg. They were watching the controls carefully, leaning over, talking to the pilots, heads bobbing up to see through the cockpit window what lay ahead, and then down again at the dials. Between the bodies, I could see their objective. The screen, gave a birds eye view of the final difficult approach, fifty foot above the rocks.

We banked again steeply and levelled, the roar from the jets building to a crescendo as the thrust reversers bit the frozen air.

Dead ahead lay the British Falkland Islands Airport of Port Stanley.

One of the standing men tensed as though sensing he was being watched. He quickly turned his head, looked straight at me and spat an angry order to the steward.

The door was closed, but he was way too late. I'd seen enough.

The 'uniforms' were Argentine Air Force – Basilio Lami Dozo's Argentine Air-Force, and they weren't out on a day trip.

CHAPTER 12

BATTLE FITNESS

"Oi, Hobbsie, Mine's a pint!" I shouted across the bar. I'd seen him going in from down the corridor as I made my way my back from the OC's office where I had passed on the good news about the crowded flight deck.

"Do I know you?"

"Oh, sorry pal." I took off the dark-glasses I had been wearing, and pushed my way through the bodies. It was pitch black outside anyway. "You know what it's like, you get used to these in my position." I scratched my head, dangled the shades and pulled a face. "Oh no, hang on though, second thoughts, maybe you don't."

"Oh it's you. You're bloody back then are you? You lazy bugger." Hobbs caught the barman's eye. "Two please mate. I thought it was bleeding Roy Orbison. Now you just look like effing Al Jolson."

Steve Chubb's horrible trademark laugh sounded behind me.

"Shit. Don't start him singing, he'll clear the bleeding bar. Make that three Hobbsie you mean bugger."

I had to grin. "Yeah, sorry pals. Had to leave the old sun bed, they needed me back here to nursemaid you two."

"Hang about. I'll rephrase my last remark." Hobbs hadn't finished. "How could I forget a face as ugly as yours?"

"Take a look in the mirror when you pass me that pint."

Chubb's macabre laugh gurgled again, "Come on then we'd better sit down." He headed off towards a free table, beer dribbling from his glass. "You poor sod Tirpitz, you must be knackered."

It was nice to be back.

At the table, I told them about what I'd seen on the plane, and gave them my take on it.

"The cunning bastards." Hobbs took a pull on his beer.

"Aye. It's that bloody simple." I said. "Don't forget, It's bastard lethal that airstrip. It's only on a narrow strip of land poking out into the sea. You try and land on it without knowing exactly how, and you'll either hit the fucking rocks on the way in or over shoot and end up in the drink on the other side."

"Yeah, he's right." Steve Chubb drained his glass. "The colder the climate the shorter the strip." He laughed. "It must have been bleeding brass monkey's when they built that one."

"So, if you reckon there were five of the bastards in there," Hobbs did some calculations on his fingers, "two flights a week makes ten." He paused then nodded, "then they could train the bastard lot in six months." He slid his empty glass towards Chubb.

"Like I said," I repeated, "it's that simple. Someone wants to start taking it seriously. The bastards come and go as they please. What's the betting some of the scrambled egg I clocked today will be over in that hacienda of theirs right now." The Argentine Embassy was built on grand Spanish lines. "I mean, if you sodding-well think about it, our security is shite. If they kick it off, there'll be bugger all they don't know about us." I banged my empty glass down next to Hobbsy's to emphasise the point. "Your turn for the wets, Chubby man."

"Jesus Christ, anything to bleeding cheer you up Tirpitz old son." He pushed back his chair and stood up. "If you carry on like this we'll have to rename you the prophet of fucking doom."

Several minutes later, he returned from the bar with two pints, clunked mine down in front of me, then went back for his own. He was right – I should lighten up. Not everyone thought as I did, but they hadn't felt the tension in Buenos Aires, how could they? I'd keep my forebodings under wraps. After all, I could be wrong, maybe Argie paranoia was catching. Whatever – it was time to change the subject.

"So, anything been happening while I've been away?" I wiped the froth from my moustache.

"Christ, yeah," Steve Chubb clattered down into the chair opposite, putting his full pint down on the wet table. "You haven't heard then?"

"Nah man, what?"

"One of the lads has bleeding cracked, hasn't he." Hobbs peered at me over the top of his pint. "Yeah, only gone and bought himself one of them rubber dolls."

"Jesus. That bad?"

"Bad enough," Chubb broke in, laughing low. "And we know where he'll be with it."

"Yeah. Straight up." Hobbs leant back in his seat until it touched the wall. "Ten to one, he'll be down the bleeding shower block with it right now."

"He's never been so bloody clean," Chubby gurgled, "the dirty sod."

"Christ, has it come to that?" I raised my eyebrows. "I thought people only bought them as a joke, man."

"So did we," Hobbs lowered his chair down and grabbed his half empty glass "but I think, with our friend it's bloomed into true love. You can ask him later, he's bound to be in." He paused for a second draining his glass. "Here, tell you what, he might even give you a go if you talk to him nicely."

"Fuck off."

"Hang on though, not so fast," Chubb laughed. "You know what they say, Tirpitz old son. Don't knock it till you try it."

I slowly lowered my glass and looked at Hobbs, both of us eyes wide.

His laugh stopped abruptly. "Don't even think about it."

At first the doll's owner would head off for the washrooms with the doll incognito in his grip but, as the word got out about his acquisition, he had nothing to hide so he started to become more relaxed. So much so, that within a very short time he could be seen in the corridors, armed with a towel, wash bag and the doll now fully inflated, tucked proudly under his arm.

It was the start of a beautiful relationship and a new face, albeit rubber, would soon be seen, making her first appearance in the bar.

Scooping up the empties, I joined the scrum at the counter, and was about to come back with the wets when I clocked Brum heading towards our table. He was laughing and pointing at Hobbsy. I caught his eye and brought back four pints.

I'd shared a room with Brum since we'd arrived on the island. Originally there were three of us but now we were down to two. The other occupant, Bob Fenson, was with us until the 'friendly' rugby match. The broken leg had bought him a ticket home.

Like most of the lads, Brum had spent a good deal of time in town after we first arrived, checking out the pubs and, more importantly, the birds. Sex, the pursuit of it, and the forbidding knowledge that we were locked on the islands possibly without any for twelve months, was foremost during most waking hours and had concentrated the mind to breaking point.

Brum was one of the fastest to score – you had to give it him. He was one of the first out of the traps and, after a few false starts he had homed in on a lady with the same thoughts in mind, who lived the other side of Port Stanley. The relationship that ensued meant that I got the room to myself on Brums weekends off. For me this meant life was better. But it was the Monday mornings after those weekends that could be the killer.

A few weeks into the romance I had the lads lined up in three ranks outside the barracks ready for our periodic Battle Fitness Training. It could be a bastard if you'd had a good Sunday night out, and the last I'd seen of Brum was at glory hour, with his lady down at the Globe.

"Where the hell's Brum, George?" Steve Chubb coughed in the cold air. It was just above freezing.

"Christ knows." I looked at my newly acquired Rolex. Five to eight.

"Last I saw of him he was rat-faced," came from down the front.

"Probably still on the job." Laughter rippled through the crowd.

"Yeah. Have you seen it? I would." There was a general mutter of approval. Brum's lady friend had a fair figure.

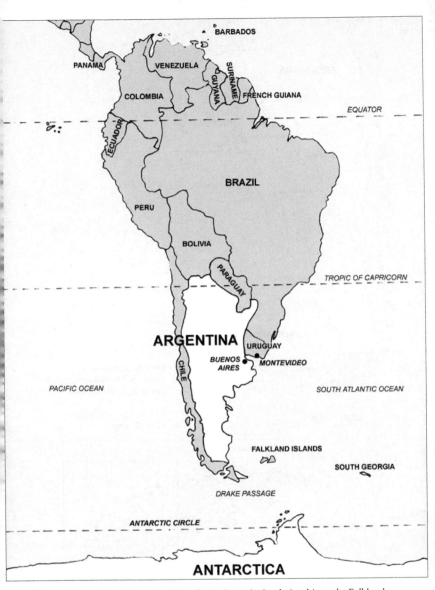

The continent of South America. Map shows Argentina's relationship to the Falkland Islands and South Georgia.

Left: Argentina and Uruguay. Map shows coastal towns and cities visited.

Below: The island of South Georgia.

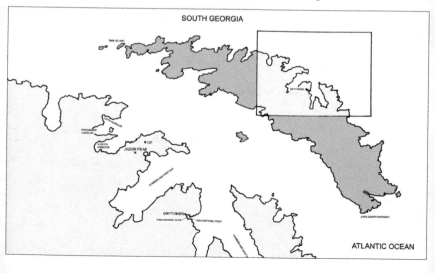

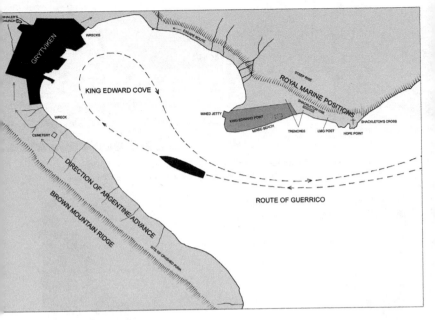

King Edward Cove.

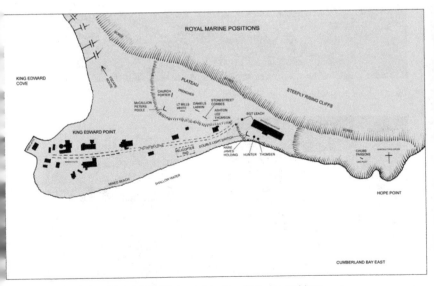

Map of trenches, King Edward Point and the Royal Marine positions.

Panoramic view from Moody Brook. Left to right: Derelict Belsen Block, Pumping Station (manned by Chileans), Wall Mountain, Two Sisters and Mount Kent behind.

Two Sisters on the skyline.

Flag above Moody Brook.

Thomsen beneath NP8901 sign at Moody Brook.

The Queen's Birthday Parade in front of the Upland Goose Hotel, Port Stanley. (Thomsen rear rank on the left, J. Noone DSM front rank.)

Thomsen, Moody Brook.

Estancia House.

Moody Brook.

Brasso's pigs.

Stormy gathering on the streets of Buenos Aires.

The Escuela Mechanica de la Armada in Buenos Aires.

Above left: Eva Peron's tomb.

Above right: Near the gates to the cemetery.

Left: The street from the hotel, Buenos Aires.

HMS *Endurance* off the coast of South Georgia.

Westland Wasp. Photographs courtesy of P. Leach.

HMS *Endurance* at derelict Grytviken, capital of South Georgia.
Photograph courtesy of J. McClaren.

Looking down onto King Edward Cove. Grytviken is in the foreground, and King Edward
Point is jutting out into the cove on the left. Photograph coutresy of Capt K. Mills

Grytviken Church.

Grytviken. Photograph courtesy of J. McClaren.

The photograph taken by Steve Martin on the morning of 3 April, 1982.
Back row, from left to right: Cpl Al Larkin, Lieut Keith Mills, Mne John Stonestreet,
Mne Les Daniels, Mne Steve Chubb, Mne Paddy Porter, Mne Laurie Church, L/Cpl George
Thomsen, Mne Jessie James, Mne Paddy McCallion, Sgt Pete Leach, Mne Dave Coombes,
Mne Spike Poole, Cpl Nige Peters. *Front row, left to right:* Mne Steve Parsons, Mne Knocker
White, Mne Steve Holding, Mne Jock Hunter, Mne Andy Lee, Mne Bob Ashton, Mne Jock
Thomson, Mne Brasso Hare.

Shackleton House. Photograph courtesy of J. McClaren.

The escape route along the open beach from King Edward Point towards Grytviken. Photograph courtesy of Capt K.Mills.

View towards King Edward Point from above Chubb and Parsons' LMG Post. Photograph courtesy of Capt K. Mills.

Benny from NP8901 detachment. Live firing 84mm Karl Gustav.

Karl Gustavs.

The 'downed' Puma on Brown Mountain Ridge.

The Argentinian Corvette ARA *Guerrico*.

Heroes return to Brise Norton. *Left to right:* Lt Keith Mills; Major General Sir Stuart Pringle, Commander in Chief of the Royal Marines; L/Cpl George Thomsen; Gerry Wiggin, Parliamentary Under Secretary of State; Butch Urand; Jerry Hunter; Brum Holden; next unknown; Steve Parsons; Steve Chubb; Bob Ashton; Cpl Steph York; Jesse James.

Thomsen in 1989 as Team Sergeant of the RM Free Fall Display Team, at a primary school in his home town of Sunderland. George had organised a parachute jump for the school.

"Come on, keep it down," I said. Then, more in hope than certainty: "he'll be here, no problem."

"Bollocks."

We still had a few minutes before the sergeant major was due to show but deep down, I couldn't see Brum making it. The silly sod must have slept in and she lived seven miles away on the other side of town. I looked down the slope in the general direction of Port Stanley where the visibility had dropped to a few hundred yards but could hardly even see the creek. With the words 'he's in the shit now' forming clearly in my mind I detected a shadowy movement in the swirling mist.

Narrowing my eyes, I squinted towards the track and picked out the form of a running figure, appearing at first like a phantom. Then, out of the gloom into full focus, came Brum, in full civvies, running like a bastard up the rise, towards the camp.

"Oi, look. It's fucking Brummy!" Rang out from the front rank.

All heads turned, followed instantly by cries of encouragement cheering him on.

"Come on Brummy, you can do it!"

"Come on my old son."

"Come on you old shagger." It was like a horse race.

His pace didn't relax as he passed the front rank. Looking straight ahead he only stopped when got to me between the men and the barracks. He was soaked with sweat and sea mist, breathing hard, and gasping for oxygen in the frozen air.

"Fucking hell Brummy," I whispered, "you've cut that fine man. Get in there and change, I'll try and stall things."

He loped off towards the door.

"We'll beat the bastard today, then," one of the lads laughed.

"No problems. He'll be knackered," another joined in.

"He's probably run all the way from his bird's place."

The guys had an idea where the lady lived.

"Yeah, he probably won't make it out of the changing room."

"He'll never do it."

There was rivalry in the ranks. Brum was undisputed champion, he was mega fit, a runner, a footballer and an athlete. But this time someone else would come home first.

Then a door slammed shut on the other side if the compound, and Sergeant Major Johnny Noon began striding through the mist towards us, with a clipboard and stopwatch.

Bollocks!

The men saw him coming and settled down. I pushed through to the front and fell them in, in three lines.

"Detachment, Detachment shn!" Heels slammed together.

"All present corporal?" Noone's boots scrunched on the gravel as he approached me.

"Detachment present and correct Sarn't Major. Err, bar one, that is, with the exception of Holden sir," I said slowly. There was a cough from the back row. Johnny looked at the back of the heads, then back to me, eyebrows raised.

"Is there a problem Corporal?" He said coldly.

"No. Not that I'm aware of sir. Holden's just in the changing room sir. He'll be ready as usual." I doubted that very much. I looked at my wrist – the seconds were ticking fast. "Fine morning Sarn't Major."

He looked at me quizzically. It obviously wasn't, in fact it was probably worse than most.

"It'll be a very un-fine morning for young Holden if I don't see him soon Corporal." He looked at me knowingly. "OK Thomsen, fall in." I moved to the back of the three lines and joined the other corporals. It would have been a miracle if the shouting had been missed in the sergeant's mess. Every one had to do the BFT. Miss it, or fail the slowest time and you were in the shit. Big time.

Clipboard held up, Johnny Noone began the roll-call, gimlet eyes falling on each Marine as they barked back their affirmation.

"Chubb? Church? Daniels?" The attendant replies came back to him. He got to Brasso. "Hare?"

Brasso scuffed his feet on the gravel. Holden's name always came next.

Noone looked into the ranks. "Hare! I know you're here, I've seen you."

"Sarn't Major!" Brasso called.

"That's better." Johnny Noone looked back down to his clipboard and made a mark with his pen. Then looked up.

"Holden?" He was met with silence. Then, on cue as he repeated the name, "Holden?", the changing room shed door slammed back on its hinges and Brum came out sprinting like a rabbit into the line.

"Sarn't Major."

A hint of a smile flickered over the Sergeant Major's face then disappeared like a ghost. "Hunter?" he said.

"Sarn't Major!" The roll call carried on like nothing had happened.

The BFT would take us on a mile and a half speed march, back towards town to the Beaver Sea Plane shed, muster there, then off, anyhow you liked, as fast as you could shift, back to Moody Brook. The time to pass your training was set at eleven minutes. My time was around eight and a half, with a personal best of eight ten. What pissed some of the faster guys off, was that Brum usually did it in seven and a half.

We set off, and more or less stayed together in the speed march, three lines like snakes, in step jog, march, jog, march, jog, march, reaching the shed in a mob, before taking off for home. Brum was just behind me, and I was pleased that he was still doing all right. We'd set off at a fair lick and by now my lungs were demanding short sharp bursts of oxygen in the thin cold air.

Running is what I did every day when I could. I enjoyed it, had done since I used to run home as a teenager from technical college in Grangetown. It's what had brought me here. My route used to take me panting past the Royal Naval and Royal Marine recruitment office on the main road. Some days I'd peer in, wondering if it was a way to beak free and leave the smoke and dirt of the shipyard job that was lined up and waiting for me. I'd leave the office behind me, cross the River Wear by the mighty iron bridge – its curved arches soaring high above the mean rooftops – then run on, on the final leg, north up Newcastle road, and home. One day, with my apprenticeship over, I had stopped before reaching the bridge.

Pushing out of the pack now, I lengthened my stride. I knew every pothole in the track. It was like playing on your home ground and at this point I'd usually done a few more miles. Knowing I had the edge, I thought about Brum's legs – they would be gone by now the poor sod. I looked round for him as I elbowed through, expecting to see him flagging but he was right there still, on my shoulder.

"How's it going George?" He rasped between breaths.

He was asking me?

"That was my question," I grunted out, as I skirted a pothole.

"Bit knackered," he puffed, spitting phlegm. "Heavy night." He splashed through a puddle. "Thanks for holding 'em up. See you back at the camp."

Lungs bursting, I put on a spurt but he was off and gone, weaving in and out of the front-runners to become lost in the icy mist.

When we got back, soaked in sweat and gasping for air, he was waiting for us. He could play all night, run six miles in civvies, then do three miles of battle fitness and still come home first. There was no doubt about it, Brum was a racing snake.

CHAPTER 13

SWIMMING WITH PENGUINS

"Here, grab these 'fore the bastards knock 'em out me 'ands." Hobbsy pushed in between the local Magistrate and his misses to drag the other tinnies off the bar.

The Globe was heaving.

He squeezed back through, beer dripping from the cans onto the floor beneath our feet, where the covering over the boards felt like it might once have been a carpet.

"Nice one!" Chubb shouted above the din.

It was number three, 12.30 pm, happy hour was half way in and the place was getting noisy.

I quaffed half, ran a hand round my chin, and lowered the tinnie while watching one of our guys push through the door and fight his way through the mob.

"Fucking brass monkeys out there." He shouted, grabbing a can.

"So what's the score, man?" I hollered.

He lowered the tinnie down, now a third empty, and belched.

"Twelve..." he thought a moment, "I think."

Hobbs looked at him sideways, shaking his head.

Chubby did his trademark low laugh. "You're a bleeding sadist my son."

"I do my best."

I'd watched the man earlier. He had been down behind the Belsen Block watching a small pile of soft nosed mullet that he had laid out a little way off on a frozen patch of stony ground.

He was a patient man, his 'roll-over' up, and his Arctic windproof zipped against the minus five, mid-July temperature. I sat and waited with him. Before long a lone gull caught the scent and began to wheel in the sky above. The seabird's cry called in more until maybe a score circled above, filling the air with noise. Slowly, they began to drop, beating in warily then wheeling up, one or two, then more until the bravest decided to land and peck warily at the Mullet.

Yes it was dead. The gull settled and began to stab voraciously. The rest fell from the sky in a hungry, fighting mob.

With the word "Excellent", the Marine joined the circuit, sending power down the two wires that snaked across the ground between us and the screaming birds. The explosion split the air – a quarter of a stick of PE4 makes a lot of noise.

Some survived, most were blown apart in a cloud of feathers, others rose then fell from the sky, wings on fire like stricken aircraft.

"Hmmm." He'd scratched his head.

Still not perfect, the angle of trajectory still needed work. He'd told me he would have another crack later. I could think of better hobbies.

"Bloody hell, look what's just come in." Chubby dragged me back to the present. He angled his beer-can towards some women by the door, and grinned at one. "It's your bird George." She was looking across, smiling at one of the guys by the bar.

"Piss off. I wouldn't touch her with yours."

A couple of the lads went over and started chatting.

"Up periscope." Hobbsy raised his tinnie, grinning. "It is who I think it is, ain't it?" he said, craning his neck."

"Don't stare, it's rude. Course it is, looks different without the coat but it's the sub alright."

Most nights the lady could be found on the quayside. She had a place nearby where she could supplement her income and in the area around the harbour there was no shortage of trade.

Chubb wasn't finished. "So, who d'you reckon she'll be going down on tonight then, Tirpitz old son?"

For recognition and warmth, the lady, wore an old yellow waterproof coat.

"Fuck knows. You're pissed enough, it'll probably be you man." I shouted across.

The coat, and her willingness to please, had won her, a nickname. To us, she was the Yellow Submarine.

His Excellency Rex Hunt pushed past clinging to a couple of full glasses. "Good afternoon men," his cultured voice cut through the din.

"Sir!"

The place had got even busier, even the elbow-room was going.

The governor disappeared into the crowd, heading for the tables.

Forty-five minutes later, we had left the pub and the tin roofed capital behind us and I was dropping out of the wide rear door of the Long Wheel Base Land Rover onto snow-dusted rock. The other five guys bundled noisily out behind.

"Christ."

"Jesus. Who's bloody bright idea was this?"

"Brass monkeys or what?"

"Come on, you've still got a couple of feet," came from the front of the vehicle.

Thump, thump. One of the lads hammered on the off-side-front wing. "Bit more. Come on. Bit more."

The exhaust stunk with the revving engine.

Whump. He hit it again. "Whoa! That's it. That'll do."

The driver jumped down, slammed the door and leaned over the wing. "Bloody 'ell. We bleedin' close enough?"

"Yeah, whack it in gear and make sure the hand brakes on. This'll be great. Make sure it's in reverse mind. We start the bastard in gear and we really will be in the shit."

I had a look at the nearside wheels. He hadn't done a bad job.

At least one of us was sober – there were six inches to the edge of the level surface, then the rock fell away vertical into the sea.

A little way back from the edge, the other Rover had pulled up, slewing to a final halt, black lines showing its progress in the snow.

The other half dozen Marines it had brought from the Globe, breath coming in white clouds, were stood in a line on the brink of the frozen rocks now, looking down into the swell.

We were on York Point, at the tip of a spit of land jutting out into the ocean on the same peninsula as Port Stanley Airport. It was a desolate place but we weren't alone. The beach, along which we'd driven, and the rocks around us were teaming with Penguins. Some were in the water beneath us. Others stood around in little groups; black wings tight into their white belly feathers, watching us, heads on one side like we'd all just escaped from an asylum.

I reached up to the gutter on the side of the vehicle and gave the cold aluminium a shove. The Rover hardly moved. Hobbs came round the side.

"He's right my son," I said, gesturing with my thumb at the guy who'd helped park the truck. "This'll make a great platform."

Hobbs looked up to the high roof then down to the surface of the sea, six feet beneath the rock, and pulled a face. "You up for it then?"

"Too right." After the warmth of the pub the minus five cold was biting hard. "Tell you what pal, it'll be bloody sight warmer in there, than freezing your bollocks off out here."

Shouts and expletives rang out from the guys around me as they began to peel off their kit.

I ripped off my jumper and shirt fast. Shit. The frost wrapped its icy tentacles round my flesh. Speed was the key. I had to get in and moving. I dropped everything and ran to the offside wing, clambered up onto the bonnet, then heaved myself up using the parallel mounted spare wheel as a step onto the aluminium roof.

The splash of water told me some guys had already leapt from the jagged rocks.

Straightening up, feeling the cold of the alli under my feet, I watched one of the guys below, running, heading for the edge of the rocks.

"Go on, me old mate," sang out.

The naked body left the edge and leapt high and out towards the water, turning a somersault.

"Watch out for that Leopard Seal," came from the rocks.

"Bastards!" The cry disappeared as the body crashed into the swell, sending up a plume of white spray.

Some of the penguins had sidled up closer to the men to see what the hell was going on. Below me, their shadows ghosted beneath the surface.

I pointed my arms and dived.

A quick rush of cold air, then I hit the water at near vertical. The southern ocean enveloped and enfolded around me.

Eyes open I kicked, down, down into the crystal sea.

Darting shapes flitted – around, above, and below me – little penguins, curious and fast, some reflecting the light in their yellow eyes from the sparkled surface high above us.

I turned, corkscrewing round in the water, and they turned with me, brushing my body and legs with their delicate pulsing wings. I pulled the water back and behind me, arms pumping, full power and kicked, like I was back in training for the County swimming championships. They stayed with me, bodies undulating rhythmically, beaks outstretched, bobbing by my side.

As we swam, a cathedral window of light cracked through from above, colouring the water a glittering green.

The sun must have broken through. We'd been shrouded in dull cloud for days. Released at last, it painted its curtain of rays deep into the oceans depths. The penguins seemed to dance in the light as they accompanied me, the swaying of their motion freeing little trapped bubbles from their feathers in a comet's tail of stars, flashing rainbow colours, past the periphery of my vision.

I headed for the surface, lungs bursting, and crashed through, taking in great gulps of frozen air.

The penguins didn't stop, their shining bodies left the water like miniature porpoises plopping in and out around me, leaving bright rings of water glinting in the southern sun. Breathing hard, I trod water, looking around, searching, but my new friends had disappeared. I was fifty yards out. From the surface you'd never know they were there, I might have been alone.

Out to sea the sun was picking up on the flat surfaces of the surrounding blocks of ice. Growlers – little icebergs – had been closing in for days. The sight of them, reminded me of the water temperature. I was right though, it was warmer in than out.

I struck out for the rocks.

A figure plunged off the Land Rover roof. Heads were bobbing in the water closer to shore.

It had to be at least one degree above.

CHAPTER 14
CHRISTMAS 1981

I'll say this for the Islanders: you couldn't fault them for their hospitality, especially during the Christmas season.

Boxing Day found me, along with Porter and Church, at a guy called Laurie Butler's house, with his wife and family, enjoying Boxing Day dinner.

It was an island tradition amongst the Falklanders to invite us Marines out during the Christmas celebrations, so all the other guys from the camp got to go out sometime over the holiday to one of the local houses as well.

It was good of the islanders. They didn't know us well, after all we'd only been on the Falklands for nine months, and yet they took us into their homes and treated us like friends.

I found it a welcome gesture. We were after all a long way from our own families, so it was a reminder of home and also a kindness you wouldn't forget.

The previous day, being Christmas Day, we'd been served our scran back at base by the officers – this was a Royal Marines tradition. Then, that night, while some of the lads went downtown for a traditional Christmas Night punch up, the rest of us had hit the barracks bar. What a piss up! The doll lost a nipple but gained a blonde wig. The last I'd seen of her she was looking good behind a bag of salt and vinegar crisps and a row of pink gins.

Not surprisingly, I was still nursing a bit of a hangover this morning as we sat around Laurie Butler's dining table.

Laurie was the chief butcher in the town's abattoir and his house was one of the best in Stanley. So as far as myself, Porter and Church were concerned, we had drawn all the right straws and that Boxing Day, sat around the dining table with his wife and two young daughters, we were being treated to roast Falkland lamb that you'd kill for.

The two girls, who looked like they were just coming into their early teens, had helped to decorate the room. Streamers hung around, and baubles twinkled in the pale sunlight filtering in through the window behind me. It was a familiar scene and that familiarity brought deep memories of childhood Christmases, back home in Sunderland, flying back to me with a vengeance.

Home. Yeah, I had some good memories but it was a long, long way away.

Eight thousand miles to be precise. It seemed to be in another time, and for certain it was definitely in another hemisphere.

I dragged my thoughts from the past, grinned across the spread at the two girls, remembering my kid sister at their age, and then at Laurie Butler, carving at the head of the table.

"You'll have a few Marines round here, man, in a couple of years," I said wanting, and succeeding to make the girls giggle. They had jet black hair and were the miniature images of his wife. She flashed her eyes towards Laurie at my chatter.

"No," he said coldly, sliding his knife deeply into the meat. "I wont."

I hung on to the grin.

You had to sympathise with a father of girls on these islands. There were few local men to go round and, anyway, who in their right mind would fancy us lot sniffing about. Touchy subject, I should have known. I changed it, and we got on just fine.

It was our host's abattoir that had finally bought Brasso's pigs off him and it was as well he sold them when he did. He nearly had to put them on castors to move them they'd grown so fat.

For all I knew, Laurie had dealt with them personally.

The craic that went round a bit later was that some of the pork on the islands that Christmas had tasted a bit different somehow, maybe just a little fishy.

But it was only a joke. Brasso's pigs would have won prizes. He'd trousered the money and grinned all the way to the bank.

That evening I met Chubb in the barracks bar, joining him on one of the plush bench seats, which were covered in cigarette burns.

"I heard the milk's back on today," he smirked, grabbing the beer I slid across the wet table.

"Yeah?" I saluted the doll, who was sat opposite, squashed between Jesse and Brum. "How's that then?" The door to door deliveries of milk around Stanley had recently ceased abruptly.

"Nobbs, my son."

"What? You mean the hierarchy?"

"Apparently, couldn't survive without it."

"So, how they getting it then? I thought the milkman was banged up in gaol?"

"Oh he is."

A group of the lads came in, one of them sidled over and placed a flat tartan cap on the doll's blonde wig.

We stopped our conversation and scrutinised the effect.

"What you think?" the Marine said, standing back, screwing up his mouth. "Hmmmm, not sure it's her colour," Jesse leaned forward and tilted the hat at a rakish angle, "but it's got something. Definitely got something."

Someone had fixed the missing nipple with black masking tape. The other one was hanging on gamely.

I turned back to Chubb. "So, they found someone else to deliver the milk then?"

"Can't do that. It's his business isn't it. No, I've heard that the nobbs have given someone in authority so much stick about not getting their bleedin' milk delivered for their cornflakes that they let the bugger out."

"What, for good?"

"Nope. And I tell you what, it could only bloody happen here." He put down his near empty glass. "Apparently the copper in the station gives the milkman the keys at night, doesn't he. So he can let himself out of gaol at three or four a.m., or whatever time milkmen are supposed to start work. Then off he trots, delivers the nobbs their milk, comes back, and locks himself up again. No bugger's the wiser, and everyone's happy." He finished his beer and did his low horrible laugh.

"Unbelievable." I said, but it had the ring of truth.

Chubby was right, it could only happen in the Falklands.

CHAPTER 15
FEBRUARY 1982: THE SWAN RUN

Some of us were a long way from the Falklands, the day once again breaking grey and wet, with salt spray and rain hammering on our ship's galley windows, as we hit yet another trough in heavy waters. We had been heading southwest now for four miserable days. A few more nautical miles and we would be where two great oceans meet – Cape Horn.

"Who's idea was this Les?" I made a grab for my plate as the *Endurance* slid down another valley of water.

"I thought it was yours, mate." Les Daniels shoved in another mouthful of breakfast.

"Whoever's it was, I hope it's bloody worth it." I pinioned my plate with my arm and lifted the mug of tea. The place was full and noisy with the clatter of dishes and chattering matelots eating lunch.

"They any better idea how long we'll be down here then?"

"Na. Can't tell." I'd spoken to the Bosun just after breakfast in the corridor.

"Depends on the conditions and how far spread out they are. The big ones should get through alright, but it's the little ones, and the stragglers, that they're worried about. If it cuts up rough and the storm they're predicting hits us, we could be down here for days."

"They must be bloody barmy!" He grinned, clutching at the rim of his sliding plate as we came out of the trough. "Still we'll be alright on this old tub." he hit the table then lifted his tea. "Then it's up the coast for us, my old mate, for sun, sea, beer and birds."

"Lead me to it, man." I raised my mug in salute.

We were both owed weeks of local leave which we hadn't taken. Like me, Les Daniels – explosives expert and Cockney optimist – could see little point in taking a holiday on the Falklands. So practically all eleven month's allowance had been building up for the pair of us since we'd arrived. We had also both got wind of the run we were now on.

We had heard that the *Endurance* was leaving the Antarctic, calling into Stanley and then heading off for a three and a half week refit on the Argentine mainland. To the uninitiated it would sound pretty boring. But, it was where the refit was, that was important.

However, as always, there was a catch: before reaching the yard we would first have to head in the opposite direction, to the south, which was precisely what we were doing now. At this first destination our job was going to be simple. A few days standing off Cape Horn as guard and rescue ship for the Round The World Yacht Race, then it's back up the coast to the Biaritz of South America, to the City of Mar Del Plata.

Once there, the *Endurance* would share the harbour adjacent to the marina with the Round The World racing yachts, for a total of three and a half weeks. The big red ship, whilst undergoing repairs, would serve as a floating bed and breakfast for us, and – and this was the best bit – the marina was next door to the most exclusive resort, with the finest beaches, bars and clubs in Argentina. Jackpot! This was a 'Swan Run'.

We picked up our plates and walked uphill towards the serving hatch as the big ship climbed the next swell. The sound of smashing crockery came from the kitchen behind the counter. Sarcastic cheers sounded round the busy room.

"Alright in there John?" I leaned across the Formica top. I'd known John Stonestreet who was one of the guys working in the galley, since our time in 41 Commando.

"Is it Hell." he swayed on the rising floor, wiping sweat from his face with a smudged white sleeve. "If it gets much worse, this place will be a bloody nightmare."

Another chef chased a clattering ladle across the floor. We headed for the door and left them to it.

Outside was the long artificially lit steel passage that formed the main artery of the boat-deck. Several matelots were still heading for the galley, Marine Al Larkin pushed passed them and headed our way.

"Oi, oi, men, fancy a tinny for later?"

"Aye, sounds good. Where's the Goffer Waller then, man?"

"Just down here." he angled his head in the direction he was walking. "I'm off down there myself."

Like John Stonestreet, Al was one of the ship's Royals.

The Goffer Waller, a little yellow man, had set up his counter a bit further along. The wooden-stepped rack he used to display his stuff, had seen hard service, in fact it was a bit of kit you'd expect to see in a tatty corner shop. The corners had rounded and splintered years before, and it was decorated with out of date stickers that curled from the grubby cracked veneer. But it served its purpose, and the little guy, underneath his Bobby Charlton haircut, grinned hopefully from behind.

He'd stacked his shop high with Mars Bars, sweets, peanuts and crisps, and along the back with his cans of beer – the tinnies. I took two Heinekens and handed over the coins. The little guy took the money, grabbing his display and steadying the toppling goods with his other hand as the ship shuddered and fell into another trough. With the action of the ship the counter wobbled and shook some packets loose, tipping sweets onto the floor.

She then steadied and rolled slowly to port then rose again.

"Christ, Les," I pocketed the beer and straightened up as the deck levelled, "is it getting worse?"

"Jesus! You tell me. Chartroom's up ahead." He gestured towards the door on the other side of the Goffer Waller. "Come on. We can take a look at it from in there."

Inside the large chartroom, the windows in the steel starboard wall looked out onto a grey sky. The ship, coming up from her cork-screw to port, had levelled on the top of the swell and was now sliding slowly into a chasm in the ocean on the starboard side. In ultra slow motion we descended and, as we dropped, the sky through the windows began to be replaced, inch by inch, like a shutter being drawn up over the glass, by an advancing mountain wall of grey water. Down, down we drove, twisting into the mighty wave, until its onrush engulfed the sky, taking the light from the room.

And then we hit.

"Shit. This wasn't in the brochure!" Les hollered, trying to keep on his feet. The *Endurance* shuddered and reeled with the explosion of the wave's violent onslaught. Our windows were underwater and the great ship was thrown to port with a creaking of tortured steel plates. We hung on to the chartroom tables as the deck moved beneath us.

Out in the corridor it was pandemonium. The Goffer Waller was in big trouble. From the periphery of my vision I caught a snapshot of the little yellow man sliding past the door after his makeshift shop.

Loose sweets, packets, chocolate bars and tinnies were bouncing and clattering in every direction around the long main corridor. He'd lost the lot.

Slowly our bows lifted, water draining reluctantly from the glass, revealing a darker ominous sky, before we fell, again roller coaster into the next grey trough. We were crossing the Scotia Ridge; an umbilical cord of submerged mountain peaks stretching across the bed of the ocean to rise again, a thousand plus miles to our east, in the inhospitable grandeur of the islands of South Georgia.

Unimpeded by land, the cold current of the southern pacific was busy beneath us, powering its way through the funnel of the Scotia Sea, the narrowest spot between 'the end of the world' (Cape Horn) and the Antarctic peninsula. It was four hundred miles of ferocious water. At 56 degrees south we were battling through the 'furious fifties' and were heading inexorably into the maelstrom of Drake's Channel and the storm-force winds of the 'screaming sixties'.

There was no let up. The storm winds seemed to increase in ferocity during the night, howling through every portal of the *Endurance*'s tall white superstructure, making sleep near on impossible. The storm and the motion of the tortured ship punctuated my waking moments and the constant drip and splash of sea water leaking into the bunkroom drilled deep into my dreams. The sea had found a way in and in the small hours had been running down a tangle of steel pipes hanging over one of the bunks, which for some reason had been built on top of the lockers. The wooden high-sided bed had finally overflowed, cascading the salt water down onto the deck beneath, forming a puddle of salty brine. The matelots called the locker bunk 'the floating coffin'.

By the morning of the following day, we had crossed well over the underwater ridge, which meant that the crazed ocean had changed its mood, dropping the unpredictable short steep rogue waves, for the longer towering mountains of the deeper water that we were now rolling into. If we could have made headway here the motion of our thrust would have driven us through, making the motion of the ship more bearable. But we had a waiting and watching brief so our engine was being used just to keep pace with the powerful current. It was a crazy situation; and treading water in the monumental seas put us at the mercy of the elements.

Lunch came and went, and John was right, it was a nightmare. The chefs couldn't work in the gale force conditions. So from now on it was pot mess, a kind of tatty-hash chucked in high-sided tins. We clung on to them. If the containers didn't bounce off the table with the plunging of the ship, then they'd be sliding around and you'd be eating someone else's scran. It was murder, but we needed the food in our guts to get us through the afternoon. The Swan Run was now looking decidedly dodgy, and to help us feel great about our decision to join the ship, we had been ordered to take the next duty on watch.

"You ready, Les?" I had my hand on the outside passageway door catch.

"I'll do." Les Daniels was barely visible under his yellow Souwester hat and high collared jacket. I was wearing the same.

I knew what was gunning for us outside, so I'd waited until we'd risen up on the next great pile of water before going out into the elements. "Come on then, Captain Birdseye." I shouted, and threw open the door.

Shite!

As I pushed out, the squall hit me, magnum force, snatching at the heavy yellow coat, trying to pick me up and throw me back towards the ship's stern. We were heading dead on into the gale. Frozen salt spray stung my eyes. A howling rage filled my ears. Les followed me out, clinging to the rails and fighting against the fierce wind. We headed for the steel stair that would take us up to the bridge – the onslaught caught in my throat making me cough for air, like it was trying to push the breath back into my lungs.

Once in the lee of the Bridge wing, we fought our way up the flooded steel stairway, one handhold at a time, gripping tight like mountaineers onto the icy steel rails. Then the ship rolled down the side of the monumental swell and a wall of freezing dark water crashed on top of us, trying to pluck us off.

I turned my head away from the deluge to see the water flowing off Les, cascading down onto the passageway beneath like a white-water river. The wing deck was awash and the lifeboat, straining on its davits behind us, poured water like a curtain from the keel of its white hull. We crossed the steel floor towards the light that shone from inside the spray lashed bridge door, and crashed through into the comparative warmth within.

One of the ship's Royals – Spike Poole – turned to greet us as we stood panting just inside the steel door. "Turned out nice again." he said.

"Aye, cracking." I said, water was flowing off me and Les onto the command centres deck. I cast around to get my bearings.

The place was packed with instruments. Another Royal was watching intently through the port windows, and a Naval officer clung to the wheel in the centre of the bridge.

"What's happening then, man?" I looked at Spike, whilst slapping water off my hat. I needed to know just what exactly we were 'watching' for.

"You mean apart from the fact we're like a fucking submarine?" He inclined his head towards the big bridge windows. I dripped across, grabbed the console and took my first look out. "Jesus Christ!"

"Bollocks!" Les Daniels had followed and waggled a finger in his wet ear.

Our view was out past the tangle of lifting winches and through and under the high converging crows nest masts on the foredeck, towards The *Endurance*'s bow. We were heading down from the crest of one monumental wave, rolling and yawing in a corkscrew motion, directly into the wall of the next mountain of grey sea. My grip tightened. We hit the wave and kept falling – the bow and foredeck completely submerged and slipping further under the ocean.

The sea flooded over the ship's deck, flowing and rushing in white wind-lashed foam, then, hammered the bridge, licking round the wings. It was level with the floor beneath our feet. The steel door creaked, twisted in its frame and crashed open with the onslaught. The storm hammered in. One of the Royals grabbed the flailing steel and heaved it to with his back.

Knuckles white I gripped the console as we gut-wrenchingly slid on, twisting to starboard, riding under the wave.

Then slowly the motion began to change. The wave that had pitched us downhill had reached the stern and we were beginning to level, rolling to port, water draining in avalanches from every gunwale.

The bow rose again; the *Endurance* emerged. The sea had lifted us like a toy, and the valley of the swell was now directly amidships. Then the ship hogged, creaking with the strain as the sea moved under us.

I hauled my eyes from the window. Spike grinned at me. "See what I mean, it's bleeding madness. We hit a wave like that every few minutes." He grabbed his yellow waterproof hat from a peg. "You know our orders chum. We're supposed to be watching for icebergs and checking the little ships as they come past, but you can hardly see a poxy thing in this."

A stronger, howling gust struck the bridge, driving water from the windows upwards in vertical lines. We were nearing the crest of the next giant hill of water and Drake's Passage was laid out grey and murky below us.

"There's one now. Crazy bastards!" He pointed past the uniformed wheelman to the huge seas on the port side of our rising bow.

I squinted into the gloom. Rising over a crest, a seventy footer was cutting through the water like a scimitar.

Faster than the waves, leaning at an incredible angle, she was hurtling along, driven by the gale force winds at a break neck speed. She disappeared into a valley. I searched the sea. Then she rose again, her high mast quivering with the power of the storm. Roller coaster, she flew, nearly leaving the water across the next swell, swooping back down in an explosion of spray, before leaving it swiftly behind with her greyhound pace.

Four crew, in bright orange jackets and day glow yellow hats, were clearly visible on deck as she hurtled past. One raised an arm in salute as they flashed past the port windows.

"They must be bleeding crackers." It was Les grinning up at me. "Fucking going some though, weren't they my son."

It had to admit it was an impressive sight.

"Aye, they've got some bollocks, I'll give them that."

Spike Poole and the other Royal left whilst we were cresting and sagging on the next swell. The bridge had filled with the sound of the howling storm. Then the door banged shut and they were gone.

It was now our job to keep watch. I watched the officer at the wheel make a few minor adjustments to keep us into the wind, then looked out at the horizon for the small ships, but my eyes were drawn once again to the bow.
Shit. We were beginning another corkscrew under the next wave.

Les had also turned his attention back to the seas that were engulfing us.

"It's a fucking good one isn't it." he said, "I mean, out here to keep watch?" The bow disappeared again into the wall of frozen water. "If any bastard needs rescuing, it's us, man."

Achingly slowly, the ship creaked under the weight of frozen water gushing across our decks, then fought back and emerged once more, only to begin the whole gut-twisting business over again.

The two race leaders had come through neck and neck earlier. The Dutchman, Van Rietschoten, and the determined New Zealander, Blake, fought it out to the finish line in Mar del Plata just a few days later. In the 6,745 miles of open sea already covered they had rarely been far apart, crossing each other's paths four times in their battle for victory.

The race had really grabbed people's imagination back home, we knew that. It really started with Maggie Thatcher removing the naval facility at Cape Town from berthing the yachts – due to her having signed the Gleneagles treaty banning sporting contact with South Africa. She'd also banned her Ministers from attending race functions and even allegedly asked doctors and dentists not to get involved!

But it went ahead regardless. Of the 29 entries, including former Para, Chay Blyth, not all would finish the course. Many had already dropped out before reaching the Horn. Some arrived already in trouble and beat through on a wing and a prayer, others were smashed in the storm.

We watched little ship after little ship, tattered and broken, limping past in the prevailing winds and massive seas. One turned a complete 360 degrees in the waves before emerging again, cracked and in trouble, but still afloat. The crew fought the storm winds to keep her on course, and managed to repair the split leaking hull beneath them. Iced water flooding in, they used her bags of plaster of paris, stuffing the fast drying powder down into the gushing holes, and successfully kept her afloat until the finish line.

One of the last through was the Italian entry. She had been boarded by an Angolan gunboat off the west coast of Africa. It held them up a little. Some of her crew were South African and they had been promptly arrested on suspicion of spying.

For four days we rode the perilous seas, battling against the unrelenting storm. Finally on the fourth day, during daylight hours, we got the all clear. The little sailing ships were all through. The announcement came whilst I was in the galley. A cheer rang out around the ship. At last for us, we could turn and leave this foul place.

The red bow swung once more northeast and we headed back with the current, crossing again over the shallow Scotia Ridge. This time, with the ripping cold flood in our wake, we passed quickly over the ships graveyard and, within fifteen hours, the gale was behind us and we were once again in the easy swell of the Argentine Basin.

The small tattered boats gamely fled before us. Our job now was to shepherd the brave little players of the world's toughest challenge back up the Patagonian coast to Mar Del Plata and safety.

Mar Del Plata, several hundred miles down the coast from Buenos Aires, was the playground of the South American rich, and to us, all that it had promised. We berthed, and tied up against the quay wall for our refit, in the same harbour enclosure as the yachts, just a short distance from their civvie marina. The Red Plum was port side on against the Quay and, behind the sheds that lined it, I could see the city golf course on higher ground. To starboard, between the *Endurance* and the South Atlantic, was a concrete harbour mole. This heavy sea defence structure ran parallel with, and in equal length with, the quay wall. Narrowing the gap at its northern tip with the marina, it formed an excellent safe deep-water mooring. The sea defence mole was maybe half a mile from our berth. Moored against it, half hidden by its shadow, two submarines wallowed in the swell, floating low in the dark water.

Beyond the Whitbread Race yachts' pontoon was the start of the fabulous beach, white and wide, stretching into the heat-hazed distance. The broad stretch of soft sand, backed onto open fronted bars, restaurants and clubs, the front entrances of which faced the main coastal road behind and the start of an exclusive row of villas. Their white facades under fancy tiled roofs peeped across the tarmac through palm shaded gardens lining the pavement opposite.

The sea fronted the western seaboard of the Southern Atlantic and was never still. It curled and broke with a constant rhythm of four-foot breakers, crashing and falling at the water's edge. These rolling waves and the strong current could spell disaster for a poor swimmer so beach guards watched from numbered towers. Higher than the beach umbrellas, they straddled the sun kissed band until they disappeared into the blue horizon at the very tip of the crescent bay. This Argentine paradise would be the playground for me and Les, plus the *Endurance*'s Marine detachment when they were off duty, for the next three and a half weeks.

Although the start of the beach was just the other side of the little ships, we had to take a tortuous route to get at it. A high wire fence ran around the perimeter of the harbour and the only way out was via the Argy guards on the gate at the southern landward corner. So it was a half mile walk, doubling back on ourselves, every trip. If we'd kept walking along the road heading south, then we'd find ourselves in Docktown.

Towards the end of our stay, Les Daniels found me on the beach.

Maria, one of the beach girls, chucked me a towel from the raffia mat by her sun-bed as he approached. Her broad mouth flashed me a smile, then she lay back down, and lifted her English magazine.

I'd recognised Les coming over as I came out of the surf. He had been walking across the sand from one of the café bars, looking at the reclining bodies.

He dropped down on a spare towel and stood a chilled six-pack in the shade of the beach umbrella. "Here, what's this about you taking a duty from Al then George?"

I rubbed my hair. "Yeah, tomorrow, said I would. He wants to go out on one of these Gaucho Ranches. Said I'd stand in for him."

I dabbed the towel around. The sun and salt weren't going to burn me now; after three weeks in it I was the colour of burnt sugar.

"What's he want to do that for?"

"Chance in a lifetime apparently. They teach you what it's like to be a real ranch-hand, you get to ride a horse with the gaucho's, you know, out on the prairie, somewhere way inland, and how to lasso steers on a real 'round up'." I folded the towel and dropped it on the mat. "Sounds great man."

"What a Cowboy." Les cracked open a tin.

Fact is, I didn't mind helping Al out at all, it would make a change to do a spell of duty.

Sand blew across, kicked up from the feet of a bunch of Royals down wind – punching the hell out of a ball. The dust pattered as it landed on Maria's magazine. She tutted something in Spanish, shook the pages and turned onto her other side. I went across to join the game.

From day one we'd been joined on the beach by the local girls. It seemed as if they were drawn in to us, like filings to a magnet.

I guess we were a novelty to the senoritas. A flash of a Latin smile and that was it – they were 'in'. It was a real catalyst to our testosterone. Most of the guys were crazy at the best of times but put a skirt in front of them and things got pretty wild. Our money was good and a night out with the lads was a pretty hairy experience. We played as hard as we scrapped. Shitfaced, hung over mornings on the beach recharged the batteries for the next night on the town. The girls got good value, a good time, and a thing most of them wanted to gain – our language. They were desperate to learn English, and in particular to speak it first-hand with the natives of our country. Fair exchange. God knows though, Maria's English, intonated with her South American Spanish lilt, then spoken with a Sunderland accent, was a strange and wonderful mix.

The girls also knew that we'd soon be gone. They'd have their forbidden fun outside the restrictions of their guilt-ridden South American Catholicism, then we would sail away, no regrets. And here's the best of it: they also knew that we were unlikely ever to return.

Good set-up. It didn't make us the most popular people amongst the Latin guys on the beach, but we could live with that.

I squinted upwards from where I stood on the quay, under a cupped hand held against the blue cloudless sky. The ship's derricks screeched, changing tone as they took the strain. I was waiting for the 'Pussers' Land Rover. Something had cropped up in the middle of Al's, shift and I was needed elsewhere.

Slowly the heavy vehicle wobbled upwards from the deck and began to swing over the gunwale towards me. Her shadow swung with her, striping the red hull, then falling onto the hot, bleached concrete of the quay's wide boulevard. Sweat stained my 'stone shirt'. The uniform was coming as a shock after nearly three weeks in civvies; it clung to my chest in the heat of the mid-morning sun's onslaught.

Two matelots were on the concrete, one signalling to the ship's derrick operator.

"Swing her out. Swing her out." he pulled the palms of his hands chest high towards his vest. Chains rattled as they fed through the ratchets. A gull screamed from the antennae masthead high above us all, mimicking the high geared machinery.

I was on a mission down town into the heart of the big city. The shadow eclipsed the sun, then the big four-wheel-drive, swaying, lowered gently onto the hard standing. The straps sagged, fell loose and the two matelots busied themselves. I pulled the directions and the city plan out from under my arm, unfolded the paper and looked again, memorising the route.

"There you go chum," the one with the mouth shouted across, slapping the curl of the aluminium bonnet. "All yours mate."

They coiled up the strapping, and headed back towards the gang-plank, shouting something to the guy on the derrick winch. I gave the thumbs-up sign to no one in particular, and walked across the concrete to the driver's door.

Within minutes, I was watching the armed Argentine guard through the rear view mirror, closing the perimeter fence gates on my smoke. Easy so far. I slammed her into third and rocked past the end of the high wire fence and then the little ships tied up in the marina on my right hand side. Half a mile and I'd hit the city traffic.

A bus came the other way, it was disorientating, I slowed and jerked the wheel. Reading maps and memorising landmarks was my stock in trade – I'd find the hotel no problem. But driving on the wrong side of the road wasn't. No point in telling them I'd never done it before, they'd have only taken the piss. I pulled the off side tyre out of the gutter, snicked the Land Rover into top gear and motored on. I was soon off the main beach artery road and fighting through the traffic-heavy streets of the modern city centre.

Twenty minutes later, I pulled up outside the big hotel, brakes squealing in the heat, switched the engine off and slammed the door. Not a bad looking place; the usual fancy flowers and a shady-looking foyer. I headed in. I was right, it was cool inside; I let the glass door fall shut behind me and looked about, eyes getting used to the light. There were people about and a desk with a smart looking senorita behind it studying her nails. I ignored them and waded through the carpet to a couple of guys sat near a pile of flight cases.

One of them looked up as I approached. "Hallo mate. You the driver?"

"Ten out of ten." Well you don't get many Royal Marines, in uniform, in Mar Del Plata.

He grinned and held out a hand. He was one of the camera crew that I'd come to collect, and they'd soon be missing the heat.

"This the lot?" I gestured to the mound of cases and pictured them filling the wagon.

"Yep. That's the kit plus the ladies."

"Yeah? Cindy Buxton and Annie Price isn't it?" I didn't know much about them but I knew their names, that they were joining the *Endurance* and sailing with us when we left port. "What are they going to be doing then man?"

"They're off back down to South Georgia for their latest wildlife film." He picked up a case, turned and looked up at me. "You stationed on the Falklands?"

"Don't remind me." My leave seemed to be trickling away fast.

"Well, they've made two wild life films there in the last couple of years for Anglia Television. You know, for their Survival series. It's been well received."

"Serious stuff then?" I nodded.

"Amongst the best. Now they're filming closer to the Antarctic."

"Jesus man, gets a bit rough down there."

"Yep, lonely too," he paused. "Anyway, lets get this stuff on board. They should be back any sec."

I grabbed a case and headed for the door.

On cue the two women arrived and between us we heaved the heavy cameras and cases into the back of the Land Rover. Then, like sardines in a can, every vent and window open, we sweated our way back through the hot, busy city centre streets, to the relative calm of the long crescent beach road.

A cool welcome breeze blew in from the ocean, a left turn from the main drag, the usual fuss with the guard at the gate, and within thirty minutes we were carrying the film crew's cameras up the gang plank of the big red and white ship. In just a few days, our new passengers safely on board, we would once again be heading south.

CHAPTER 16

THE MEN FOR THE JOB

March was nearly over, and we would soon be on our way home. So it was kind of party time. We'd been invited out to one of the islander's houses, and although the beer was still flowing we were on our best behaviour.

In fact, we only had another nineteen days to go before we headed off. These were really nice people, and it was good of them to throw us a farewell party.

"You like these, eh George?" Jim, the owner of the house, said over my shoulder.

"Aye, they're good." I meant it. He wasn't just a nice guy but a fair artist too. Maybe I was going to buy one of his pictures to take home.

There was a shout of laughter from the tussle round some of the attendant local girls, on the other side of the big room. One of the lads had fallen over the back of a sofa. I threw them a look, then turned back to the canvas.

"Don't worry about the mess George." Jim's missus must have seen me eyeballing them as she came alongside me, holding out a tray of food. I took a couple of sausage rolls.

"They're bound to be a bit silly now and then, they're only boys – probably counting the days now as well." She bustled round to the mob pushing in amongst them.

A bit silly? Now and then? How about all the times when there was totty around? Then, the only thing on their minds would be the girls they were trying to pull. I turned back to the canvasses and stuffed in a sausage roll.

The pictures fascinated me, but the truth was that it was a bit more than a maybe that I'd buy some. I'd more or less decided on taking a couple home but I'd strike the deal sober – this wasn't the time. They were different, kind of *Lord of the Rings* fantasy-ish and maybe that was the attraction. You expected to see a Hobbit hiding somewhere in the brushstrokes. So they'd be like a souvenir. The island was full of them, Hobbits I mean. I looked at Jim, he'd escaped and was quite normal, but Tolkein would have been proud of a lot of them: little short bodies, thick arms and legs with red swollen faces. We thought it was either genetic or a result of booze and the weather.

I stuffed the other roll in and one of the girls squealed, followed by Chubb's dirty laugh. Then I heard the front door.

Jim looked at me. "Expecting any more George?"

With a mouth full of crumbs, I shook my head. The door had been opened to Murray Patterson, duty driver, in rig. He stood framed in the doorway, sober, looking round the room till his eyes rested on me. Then he mouthed something across the noisy room and hooked his finger. There was something about him that told me it could be serious. But if he'd spoken I wouldn't have heard him for the catcalls and piss-taking from the lads.

Crossing the room to him was like running the gauntlet, so when I got to the hall I closed the door on the noise.

"What's up Murray man?"

"Sorry George." He looked at me oddly. "But you're wanted back at camp, old son."

"Piss off Murray, man. This is a fucking wind up, right?" I said the words but there was something about him that told me I was wrong.

"Honest, George, no fucking around. The boss wants you back. Now."

"Shit!" It wasn't my call, I wasn't on duty. Why the hell would he want me?

"So what's going down?" I asked. It had to be someone pissed-up or a punch-up was going on somewhere and they needed some back up.

"I don't know much about what's happening myself George," he said quietly, scanning the empty hallway and pausing. "But I do know this much. And this time its no fucking wind-up. The Argies have kicked something off and the rumour is that the shit is about to hit the fan."

Bollocks!

I went back in, said goodbye to our hosts then turned to the lads, my expression a dead giveaway to the ones less pissed.

"Right, come on lads, that's it, knock it on the head, we've got to go."

"Piss off."

"Get stuffed," came from the back and one of the girls giggled. I could do without that. I moved closer and changed my tone. I wasn't too pleased either.

We thundered down the pot-holed track in the four-tonner, pulling into the compound with a squeal of brakes and diesel smoke. No point in telling the lads why we were back, after all I only knew what Murray had told me. I'd know more after seeing the boss. Just "something going down" was enough for now. I jumped down from the cab as they pitched out the back, arsing about, shoes scrunching across the loose grit, making for the bar. Maybe the night air had sobered them up a little, but they'd soon catch up. It was a shit way to end a farewell party. I went for a shower.

Fifteen minutes later, I was in the wardroom doorway feeling pissed off that I'd bothered to wash away the smell of booze. They were sat drinking, looking relaxed, still in civvies, doing the 'officer' act.

"Come in Thomsen." It was the OC Garry Noott. He put down his glass and stood up. "Close the door." He raised his eyebrows. "Get you anything? Drink? Cup of tea?"

Yeah, fucking right. I'd been hauled back, I was in uniform and obviously back on duty. Tea would taste like piss after the beer.

"No thank you sir. I'm fine."

"As you like." he sat back down and waved at one of the leather studded armchairs. "Grab a pew. Am I right in thinking you've met Lieutenant Mills?" He was the only other occupant. He nodded as I parked myself.

"Aye, sir." We'd met a few times in the gym. He was Officer In Command of the Marine detachment on the *Endurance*. He was a bit younger than me, medium height, not heavy but super fit, a black belt, a boxer and a mountaineer, with the kind of eyes that looked right through you, deep set and bright. He was born for the job.

"Right then. Now, Thomsen, thanks for coming back."

Like I had a choice?

Garry Noott cleared his throat. "It seems we have a problem in South Georgia. Heard of it?" he looked up, saw my nod and carried on. "Then you'll know that it's a freezing British outpost of mountains and ice, eight hundred miles south-east of here, damn near in the Arctic Circle.

From the information we have, and it's a bit sketchy still, it appears that the Argies are up to their old tricks again and this time things could very well go off." He paused. "This much we know: a scrap metal merchant, name of Davidoff, has landed at Leith Harbour, one of the old disused whaling stations, without the proper protocol. There's a British Antarctic Survey Station in Grytviken, just along from Leith and he knew damn well that he should have registered there first." He swilled the puddle of piss-coloured liquid around his glass.

"Now, we're getting our information from the guys that man the station. They're a pretty tough lot, and no fools. According to them, they have been round to see what's going down and been met with a pretty hostile response. They report a presence on shore that look more like Marines than scrap merchants. Davidoff's men are swarming all over the place and shots have been fired. Not only at the protected herds of reindeer for meat but possibly at the scientists as well. Apparently some shots have passed too close to be a coincidence."

Christ. Nineteen days and I'd be on the boat home.

"And they've raised the Argentine flag."

Not now.

He leaned back and sighed crossing his arms, "so you see Thomsen, the situation is grave and that's why we've brought you back."

I nodded, like I didn't think it was a bad dream.

"Yes sir." Come on then, let's hear the worst.

"I want you to take a detachment down to South Georgia with Lieutenant Mills and his Marines to sort the situation out."

My mind raced. Why were we all hauled back from town? "Which men sir?"

"Your men George, your team and a signaller. Take Church for that, plus whoever else you think you'll need. Who you choose is up to you. I want you to pick your own team for this one." Mills nodded his agreement.

Noott carried on: "We haven't long. We sail in the morning." My Rolex told me that was just under two hours away. "Any who you'd want Thomsen?"

Easy. I wanted the best. "Yes sir, I can tell you their names now."

"Good."

I didn't have to think about it, I knew the men I'd need – every one. They had one thing in common. They had bottle and would have the will to get in the fight. "Hare, James, Holden and Hunter. That's my team sir, and in addition I want Chubb, Daniels, Porter and Hobbs."

"Ah. Sorry, can't have him."

I raised my eyebrows.

"No, can't have Hobbs I'm afraid, he stays here. He's too useful in the mess."

Jesus Christ! Hobbs was his bloody batman, I'd forgotten how important that was. Fuck the operation, they needed their butler.

"Yes sir." I'd give Hobbsie some stick for this. The fact that he was an oppo had nothing to do with his selection or the others. He was also one of the best – I'd be a good soldier down.

Noott leaned forward, putting his empty glass carefully into the centre of his coaster. "You will, of course, be going fully armed. The gravity of the situation is such, in my opinion, that it requires you to go down with full 'war scale' ammunition. Mills will, of course, be arming his men in the same manner." He turned to Mills, eyebrows raised.

"Oh yes, we've plenty of ammo and weaponry on board sir," Mills came in, then looked at me, "enough, hopefully, to see us through if things get nasty."

Nice one. That would help. In a fire-fight, 'full war' runs out like a punctured bucket.

Noott picked up his glass again and studied it, probably wanting a refill but party pooper here was staying dry. "As well as the 'full war' Thomsen, take what else you want."

Nice of him. A few extra toys would come in handy. "Thank you sir. Then I'll be taking a few 66mm LAW rocket launchers and some 2 inch mortars, with smoke and HE as well," I gave it a second, "for good measure."

He looked up from his glass. I looked back. The Tirpitz was leaving port. And I'd make damn sure my team had the weapons to finish the job.

I left the mess and headed for the bar to find the guys. Most were sat at the corner table, Chubb and Brum either side of the doll. The new flat cap over the blonde wig was doing nothing to detract from the startled open mouth. The black gaffer, crudely repairing its nipples, didn't help much either. Lined up in front of her on the wet table, she had three vodkas and something else I couldn't put a name to, with a cherry on a stick.

Give them their due, they could tell we had business. There was no fucking around. The rumours would have been flying round the bar when we'd got back. You couldn't fart in the camp without someone knowing.

"Right lads, it's on. There's shit going off, down south, and we leave in the morning. Early." They'd all come in at that, wanting to know the score. "Nah, not here. I'll give you the details later." I rate 'a time, and a place' as one of the better clichés. "Finish your drinks. Get back to your rooms. Check your kit, thoroughly," I paused "then check it again. Get a shower. Freshen up. And, my room in one hour." I did the thumb over the shoulder.

I needed the hour to get my head round things, and to liase with Harry Dorey, the armourer. I wanted weapons and ammo, ready for collection, seven thirty sharp, after breakfast. By the time the eight men left my room, they had the same scant information that had been given to me. It was just gone midnight. March 21st 1982.

Daylight found us cold and wet, waiting on the jetty. I adjusted my beret so the rain would run off onto my shoulder instead of down my neck. Typical! It had started out cold but fine. It had been raining now for thirty minutes. Everything, piled in a small hill to our backs, was soaked. Rocket launchers, mortars and ammo. I just hoped the boxes were waterproof. A loose seal and the damp gets in and we'd have a dud. Brilliant. They always came out when you needed them the least.

We sat on our kit, huddled in the lea, waiting and watching. I opened my mouth and listened. Visibility had come down like a blanket with the rain – hundred yards max. So I knew I'd hear the launch before I saw it.

The noise, when it came, was from the wrong direction. All heads turned. I got to my feet. Two lights came first, dimly out of the fog, followed by the familiar site of the red taxi moving cautiously along the quayside. It pulled up close, the sound of the London cab diesel wheezing into silence. A black umbrella came out first, followed by the Governor. His shrewd black eyes, under his thinning grey barnet, looked tired and drawn.

A gull, calling somewhere out in the harbour, accompanied the scrunching grit as we formed a miserable wet huddle.

"Good morning gentlemen." He came in amongst us, hand outstretched pumping flesh. It was a shit statement, reminding me that he was a politician, but the handshake was sincere. Drips flew off Arctic waterproofs as he clasped each wet hand.

At the end of the line he turned to me. "Are you all here corporal?"

Was it me, or was there a hint of surprise in his voice? "Aye sir, all present and correct."

At my answer he looked down at the puddled grit, breathing out audibly, rain dripping off the shiny spikes on his brolly, then lifted his head, eyes sweeping round, like he was counting us, taking us all in.

"Right then, gentlemen." His voice was clear and concise, like a headmaster in assembly. "You will have already been briefed on the situation, so I won't confuse things." He cleared his throat. "The only information we have as to what's happening, is relayed directly to my office, from the BAS boys. I can tell you nothing has changed since yesterday. But," he gave it a second, "I suspect the situation to be pretty fluid."

Great, we'd be three days at sea.

"So we don't know exactly what you'll find, when you get down there."

What else did he know that he wasn't telling us?

"One thing I'm certain of, though, is that whatever happens you will account for yourselves well."

Dead on cue, the throaty sound of the launch began to ebb and rise through the fog.

"So gentlemen," he straightened and saluted beneath the brolly, "I wish you farewell and good luck."

Reflecting on his words, I watched the taillights disappear, while the invisible launch got louder.

That was it.

The launch appeared like a pantomime genie.

He had just said 'goodbye'.

CHAPTER 17
CHIPPING OFF

"What the hell's going on?" I hung on to the doorframe as the ship bucked. We had been two days ploughing through the heavy seas.

"What's it look like?" Chubb looked up, holding up a hammer with a chisel shaped head. "We're chipping off, aren't we?"

I'd heard the tapping of metal on metal on my way down to 'the heads'.

"Chipping off? Says who?"

Bodies popped out from the cubicles. I'd only seen two guys, Chubb and Jesse. Now I could see they were all in there.

"The Master At Arms came and got us didn't he," Brum said, from the first cubicle. "We got to chip off and paint the toilets he says."

"Have you fuck as like." I could feel my temperature rise. "Gave you an order did he?" A general muttering of expletives filled the tin room. "Well, this is an order, right? Brushes and hammers," I pointed at the tools in their hands, "over the side!"

They filed out. Chubby gurgled. "You'd best tell him then, Tirpitz old son."

"Try and stop me." I hooked my thumb at the door. "Go on. Sling 'em."

I'd wondered where everyone had been. Two days out, meant two days closer to the 'big freeze'. It was cold as a penguins arse so you wouldn't have seen them on deck and no sign of them in the mess.

In the event, Sergeant Major Pete Leach passed my views on in the Chief's Mess. He'd been present when I found Lieutenant Mills. Still fuming I made my point.

"Tell the Master At Arms something for me, will you sir?"

"Go on."

"My men are not ship's company. They are on their way to a battle zone, and this boat is the taxi. They are not his flunkies. They will not be painting his shithouse and they take their orders from me, not from a bloody matelot, Sir."

"Thank you Thomsen." Mills' piercing eyes drilled me. "You've made your point."

Leave it to me sir," Pete Leach raised his powerful frame from the chair by the chart table. "I'll see the Master gets the message."

The detachment from the *Endurance*, together with my section, had brought the company up to platoon strength. Granite hard and more experienced than any of us, Sergeant Major Leach was second in command. He took no prisoners. Job done.

Next morning morale hit the deck. Since our first day out we'd been hammering through heavy ice filled seas, flat out, intent on conflict. The captain, Nick Barker's foot had been pedal to metal since the off and the old lady hadn't flinched. Everything was at full readiness. We would be dropped by chopper the other side of the island and come across the glaciers fully armed to infiltrate Leith from behind. The *Endurance* would blockade the harbour. If she couldn't talk Davidoff's men into a peaceful surrender then we would help change their minds. That was the plan Mills and Leach had been working on it since we'd left port. What we hadn't counted on, though, was the bloody politicians.

"You can stop polishing your bullets now man." Jesse had just brought his tray across from the galley, joining us at the table.

"More's the bloody pity." He shot me a grin. "Left my bloody kit back at camp anyway. Still," he picked up his knife, "might not need it now."

His 'kit' was his personal arsenal. I looked at him over the rim of my mug. He spent hours happily making up his own hollow shells for his favourite sawn off. "You'd have only shot the shit out of everything anyway."

"True."

And it was. They kept him off the ranges – he made too much of a mess of the targets

"So what happens now?" Chubby pushed his plate away. "Bunch of wankers."

"Not Mills and Pete Leach. They'll be as pissed off as us like." Brum chimed in. He had a point, they'd be pig sick at the change of plan.

"I didn't mean them. It's the bloody politicians want to make their frigging minds up, that's who. First it's on, then it's off. Like they're playing bloody tin soldiers. Here, who did he say had called it off?"

"The FCO." I reminded him.

"Yeah, that's it, the poncy Foreign and Commonwealth Office, bottling out, typical."

Brum nodded and rubbed some bread round his plate. "Frigging 'see you next Tuesday' office, more like."

He was right. They hadn't got a clue. We were pumped up and ready and there was a lot of anger. What we didn't need right now were jumpy politicians. One day they'd cry wolf once too often.

The change in the game plan had switched channels from aggressor to watcher.

"We will now be going direct to the BAS Base at Shackleton House instead."

Mills had Briefed in the crowded galley.

It suited me. The yomp across 20 miles of mountain and glaciers could have crippled some of the guys before a shot was fired anyway, and I'd said as much to Pete Leach when the first plan was unrolled.

"The captain will maintain radio silence and be taking us in," Mills looked at his watch, "at 0645, under cover of darkness."

So it was settled; we'd land at King Edward Point in the sheltered deep water harbour of King Edward Cove, home of the boffins and a short walk from the deserted whaling station of Grytviken.

And I'd also got a job. Chubb and Church met my eyes as I scanned round the metal room. I needed radio and back up. We'd be leaving next day at first light.

CHAPTER 18
THE EAGLE'S NEST

The motion of the ship had finally ceased. Along with it went the vibration and hum of her motor. The silence was eerie. It told me we had arrived. My watch registered 06.43 when the pedal was finally lifted, reducing the engine note to a gentle hum. It was now just after seven and, with the silence still ringing in my ears, there came a faint light from outside.

I emerged on deck to the dawn. Two hours before we leave the ship and a chance to get my bearings.

"What's it like?" Chubb rubbed his eyes and leant on the rail. He'd clanged up the iron stairs from the locker room behind me.

I was still taking it in. To my right, crummy little bungalows and sheds crowded round a point with what I took to be Shackleton House, like a great two story railway shed, windows lit, looming behind. But in front was something I hadn't been prepared for. The view was humbling: a picture that seared through my eyes to brand itself indelibly inside my skull.

"Jesus Christ, mega or what?"

It was beautiful, and three days at sea no doubt helped to reinforce the surreal impact. The wind had dropped to zilch. We seemed to be parked on a mirror. In the crystal water, in perfect detail, snow capped mountains soared upwards, ending thousands of feet above in craggy peaks. Between them and the sea, white slopes ended in a little church spire behind a dark line of Grytviken rooftops.

We were surrounded by deep shadow. There was no sun in the bay – it was still hidden from us by dominant hills on the eastern side of the harbour. But it was there, above and in the reflection of the deep, and it was striking the highest peak, set God knows how many miles inland – a fire crest amid rolling clouds.

A few snowflakes drifted down as I drank in the scene. It was one I would never forget, I pulled up my collar, and followed Chubby down for breakfast.

At 09.45 next morning, it was a different place. We bundled our heavy gear into the Wasp and dived in, out of the rising squall. Church slammed the door shut with a curse.

"Turned out nice again." The pilot half turned his helmeted head towards us, grinning.

"Bollocks. What have they done with the weather?" I fished the seat belt out from underneath me.

"Not been here before then?" It was more a statement than a question.

The chopper rocked, hit by a heavy gust.

"Nah man, it was dead calm earlier."

"You better get used to it. This place is crazy. One minute the sun will be up, you think you're in heaven. Next minute a storm will hit you. It comes out of nowhere." His hand came up to his chin-strap. "Something to do with the mountains."

Chatter came over his comms. He fired the motors.

"It's not just the ice and snow that's the bastard, it's the wind. It's a bitch to fly in. You never know which way it's coming. Even comes straight down." He slammed down a few toggles and the engines made talk impossible.

Cheerful thought. I looked at Chubb and Church. They were both studying the foul weather, outside the perspex, battering the tops off the waves. Just what we need for the climb.

My stomach dropped. The pilot raised the Wasp a few feet above the poop then plunged her down over the side. We levelled up just above the waves, lower than the ships gunwales, and skidded off – forty-five degrees – full belt towards the shoreline.

He was a pro and this was the best little killing machine on the market. Fast, agile and deadly. She had wheels for feet and was capable of carrying a deadly pay-load of eight AS12 anti-armour missiles. And if you fancied a kill fest you could cram three of us in for that extra special surprise.

We clung on, the whop whop of the rotors filling our ears.

No one would see this little baby coming, or hear her, until she was on top of them. Six feet max, we contour flew, in and out of bays, banking to fit the shore-line, water buffeting the screen, wipers going like one stick drummers. It made Blackpool's big dipper feel like a teacup ride. We were out of Cumberland East Bay, past Hope Point, then round into Cumberland West, heading north to Carlita Bay at the foot of Jason Peak – our destination.

There was no ceremony, just a grin from the pilot, rotors still turning nearly lifting her off. We scrambled out, hauling the pile of equipment with us, backed off quick, staying low, left the grey shale beach and went to ground amongst the rocks. The downdraft from the blades tried to blast us into the deck. Then a hand came up in a wave of farewell behind the flailing wipers and the Wasp was airborne again – her rotor tips, as she banked and raced for the narrow craggy entrance, slashing the hell out of the waves. And within seconds, the sound and the chopper were gone.

Silence filled our ears with its tinnitus ringing. Through it came the abating wind and the bark of seals on the lower beach.

I turned and craned my neck. Above us was our destination, its crest hidden by low cloud, a gigantic lump of rock and ice, christened Jason Peak, the perfect look out tower. From the forward slope of her 2,200 foot summit, the north west of the island would be laid bare before us and in particular the bit that interested us most. We would be looking directly down onto Stromness Bay and Leith Harbour.

Jumpers off, windproofs back on, laden with ammo, weapons, radio equipment and Bergens, we hit the rock, no pissing about, this was no exercise, we wouldn't be stopping until we had reached the lower slopes of the summit.

"Perfect." I lay on my belly in the dusty snow adjusting the binoculars. We had rounded the peak just below the top, keeping our silhouettes off the horizon, finding the 'Eagles Nest' ledge just ten minutes before.

"See anything?" Chubb had dumped his gear and the tent a couple of yards back and knelt beside me on the snow. Twenty feet further down the slope the rock dropped sheer into the mist. Church was breaking out the radio.

"Perfect" I repeated.

Chubby looked across the bay at the ship I had homed in on. "Looks like a Dinky toy," he said.

To my eyes the bin's brought the scene up-close and personal.

"Take a look for yourself." I passed up the glasses and sat up, searching for my notebook.

Chubby whistled. "Not messing around are they?"

"Nope. If they're scrap merchants, I'm a fucking Chinaman."

Below us, on the other side of Stromness Bay, lay Leith Harbour; a scrap merchant's dream come true. A rusting dumping ground of half-sunk whaling ships and a tangle of derelict steel buildings. What was once a stinking slaughterhouse rich in whale fat was now rich in old iron and worth a small fortune in bronze from the ship's propellers – Davidoff's excuse for being here – but the binoculars told another story.

I scrambled back up the slope and found a flattish pitch for the tent. The site couldn't have given better cover. The jagged pile was a mix of drifting snow across ice and grey rock and, with the ridge behind us, the white tent would be invisible. The downside would be the exposure to every weather front the island could throw at us. There would be two outside at all times: one mounting rear guard and radio, the other watching the enemy. The lucky one got to eat and sleep wrapped like a slug in his Arctic bag, his boots still on. Take them off in this freeze and your feet could swell like balloons. If the shit started flying, the last thing I wanted was someone fucking around with his laces. We fought as a team, one man's comfort could cost us our lives.

It was the cold that determined everything. It decided me to work in three-hour shifts. Any more and the numbing temperature would start playing tricks with your senses. Boredom would set in and you'd get careless.

Laurie Church stopped fiddling with the radio and stood up, stretching. His legs would be aching like mine from the long fast climb.

"See much?" he asked, pulling at his rolled-down 'head over'.

"Aye, they're still at it." I nodded down at the Clansman 351. "You set up?"

"Yup. Should be fine." He squinted down past Chubb to the distant ship.

"She's the *Bahia Buen Suceso*." I answered his look, checking the spelling on my pad. "Like we thought, she's every bit an Argy Naval Transport Ship."

"Nice."

"Very. And it looks like they're bringing more stuff off than they're putting on."

The glasses had shown a hive of industry on the quayside. Some of the guys amongst the civilian workers were dressed in white and looked suspiciously like Argentine Marines.

I looked at the dial on my wrist and handed him my notes.

"Better make contact now then Laurie, then every four hours." He nodded, checking his watch. "And best keep the messages to the minimum," I threw in.

He headed back to the Clansman. There was an audible click followed by a high-pitched whine as the set came to life. If they tuned in to our frequency, they'd never bloody spot us anyway, but why let them know we were here? Best to keep it as a nice surprise. They'd find out on our terms, or not at all.

I scrunched through the fine snow towards Chubby. A gust of frozen wind blasted in, breaking the stillness, picking up the powdered permafrost and chucking it at my legs. The ship could wait. Priority-one was 'tent up' and a wet before the weather set in again.

Forty-eight hours on, we stood back down on the shale beach in the half-light of the Antarctic dawn. With a few minutes to kill we had time to go in amongst the sea leopards and giant elephant seals basking in their hundreds on the lower shore.

Nothing had changed during our watch. The industry between the vessel and the town had carried on unabated. Smoke rose in grey streaks from various fires and the Argentine flag still fluttered on the high generator tower. Apart from that, zilch, and not another vessel in sight. The mandarins back at Whitehall must have been chuffed to nuts. Our encrypted messages, scrambled and relayed home via the *Endurance*, would be music to their ears. Send us down to do a job, bottle it and hope it blows over. We'd heard it before. I wondered why it had taken them so long. The way our masters worked it wouldn't have surprised me if the *Endurance* had been called back before we'd even reached port.

I checked my watch. We headed back towards dryer ground on the upper shoreline. The chopper would show before we heard her. No burning and turning this time, she'd have time to settle. She'd have to, I needed to brief the new team she was bringing before we wave-hopped back. And for a bonus the cab would at least be warm, the first heat for two days.

Despite the roller coaster ride and the noise of the rotors, I knew I'd be fighting sleep.

CHAPTER 19

A DRINK WITH 'THE BEAR'

The following evening, we left the *Endurance* and headed round the bay towards Grytviken. The air was filled with our breath, raw with the frozen atmosphere, and punctuated with the scrunching of our boots on the scree and ice of the rough track. I carried a case of Heineken tucked under my right arm. Chubb and Laurie swung cans of lager from their fists as we homed in on our objective.

A ship had arrived under cover of darkness, and we had woken to find her sharing our waters. She was a giant Soviet rescue trawler – her excuse being the need for fresh water.

She hadn't moved since our first visit in the dawn light, floating low in the crystal water, moored like an ugly brown scab against the harbour wall. Nothing out of place there, she fitted in perfectly with the rust and squalor of what was left of Grytviken. The only other shipping had long since left. All that remained now were the rotting hulks of disused whalers lying half submerged like ghost ships where they had been abandoned.

"It's a fucking rust bucket," Laurie coughed, "look more at home in a bloody scrap yard." I studied the vessel, resting a couple of hundred yards ahead, the late sun now full on her. He had a point.

"It can sink when we've finished their vodka." Chubb looked sideways at me doing his trademark laugh. "Have to hand it to you Tirpitz, old son. You take us to some right shit-holes, but this ones even below your standard."

I shifted the case under my arm and he stepped to one side.

The scene as we approached was lit by clear sub-arctic sunlight making the rusty roofs glow like hot embers against the snow-covered mountains that towered above. Below the giant peaks, set in the bay between us, the sea was so calm that its surface reflected every detail.

As we closed in, the red rooftops became hidden behind the big ship's rusty derricks. She'd done little or nothing to disguise the tell-tale state-of-the-art antennae that probably had little to do with fishing, but a lot to do with electronic-surveillance, and auxiliary-general-intelligence-gathering, that the Soviets were good at. Couple it with the presence of the customer we'd shouted up to earlier in the day and we had the makings of a classic one hundred percent spy ship.

"Big bugger ain't he?" Chubb had laughed that morning.

"Bloody monster." I carried on waggling my hand in the age-old drinking sign at the large Soviet squinting down from the deck.

"You got a bleeding cheek," Chubb grinned. "Still, if you don't try, eh." Then joined me making the same gesture.

A grin of recognition began to spread on the broad face above us.

"Drink?" he said, and raised his eyebrows.

We waggled more, grinning.

"Da, drink." he boomed. The rouble had dropped, and a grin began to spread over his face, making him look like a large Cheshire Cat.

"You got it pal." I was pleased that I'd be getting a closer look at the ship.

"Nice one." Chubb laughed, thumbs up.

"Da. Tonight." The Soviet pointed to the deck, his grin now had grown from ear to ear.

"Here. Wodka." he said, and we held our thumbs up, satisfied with the mornings work.

"Black tie?" Chubb looked at me.

"Bugger" I said, "forgot to pack one."

When we reached the quay, he was waiting for us, beckoning us up the gangplank and grinning like a ringmaster. He'd looked big from the quayside that morning but now on deck and level with him I could take in the full extent of the man. His bulk loomed between the three of us and the bridge, filling the gangway. We held up our cans of Heineken to show we were friendly.

Black, highly polished boots, black full-length great coat wrapped around his power-lifter shoulders, topped off with a black fur hat, gave him the appearance of a large bear. One thing for certain, despite the smell emanating from the ships hold, he was no fisherman. KGB was stamped all over him. He wore it like a badge.

"Hey, English," he boomed, taking my outstretched hand with one great paw and squeezing my upper arm, like an old friend, with the other.

I could sense the power of the man. His slits of eyes beaming down at me above high cheekbones.

"So. You work out huh?" He stepped back and slapped my shoulder. It was like a playful kick from an ox.

I held his look for a few seconds, playing my part in his game, then nodded. "It's been known."

"Hah, good." He beamed a bit wider. "We will get on, my friend."

He turned to the others, crushing their hands.

As he spoke, a uniformed officer appeared from a door and came across, attracting his attention. They talked rapidly in Russian.

While they talked I looked around me. From our height on deck I got a new angle on the town. Between the rusting rooftops and a row of great round storage tanks was a view of a little hill, climbing behind before rising sheer at the foot of the mountains. On it was built a tiny church. But, unlike the deserted town, it appeared to be well maintained. The white walls dazzled in the last rays of sunlight and its little spire glowed redder and brighter than the Communist star implanted in our new friend's bearskin hat.

"Come. Follow me." The big man had finished his conversation and turned his attention back to us. His breath hung in the air in the failing sun like a small cloud.

"I show you round my little ship." The grin came back, "then we have drink."

The other man had stayed to hear the statement. He now walked off, nodding in our direction from underneath his large hat. They had obviously decided the booze could wait. Fine by me. It was the ship that interested me anyway.

We headed amidships, stepping over heavy hoses being run ashore by two or three crewmen jabbering in Russian. I took note: the pipes disappearing amongst the buildings headed up hill in the right direction, toward the fresh-water stream that had once fed the town. It confirmed nicely the reason she had given for her presence. At least they were making an effort.

We reached the bridge. I followed the big guy up the narrow checkerplate steps, gripping the rusty safety rail worn smooth with use. His rubber soled boots squeaked on the frosty steel. He turned on the half landing then stooped through the watertight door, and we shuffled in behind.

Inside was like Aladdin's cave. More like the bridge of a warship than a trawler. I scanned around. Every conceivable space beneath the square, salt encrusted widows, was packed with steel grey cabinets bristling with high tech sonar, radar, communication equipment and other instruments that we could only guess at the use of.

It was obvious that we were aboard one seriously high tech boat. I blew out in a long whistle. The big man liked it, throwing out his right arm in a showman gesture. "You see here, my friends, a fine Russian fishing ship." Then he grinned his Cheshire Cat grin again, but the smile didn't reach his eyes. "Is good. Da?"

"Aye, you've got some fancy looking kit here pal." Laurie Church, signaller and communications expert, scanned the equipment stacked around the room and confirmed my opinion.

"Yeah. It's the dog's bollocks alright." Steve Chubb winked.

We left the command centre to be shown around the working deck of the vessel, to which the bridge was in stark contrast. From what I could make out from our guide's broken English, she was supposed to be some kind of fishing fleet recovery ship, which the powerful lifting derricks, winches and cutting gear littering her decks seemed to bear out. I've been around ships since a kid, serving my apprenticeship as a welder on Sunderland Docks and I knew a heap when I saw one.

At first glance she gave the appearance of needing rescuing herself. Paint flaked from the superstructure and great stains of rust ran like zebra stripes down her plating. I thought at first that I wouldn't have gone out in her on a boating lake. However, on closer inspection I could see that the rust was only superficial, almost as if it was part of her livery – hiding the real ship beneath. Maybe she looked like a wreck because that's how the Kremlin liked it.

In fact, I'd seen ships of her kind before, but never this close. She would be a part of one of the fleets of Russian Trawlers to be found on the high seas almost anywhere in the world at any given time.

We now know that they numbered possibly in their thousands at the height of the Cold War. A formidable armada by anyone's standards and this one was probably a bit bigger than most – I'd say about a hundred and sixty feet. The cutting gear and winches she carried would have been used to keep her smaller boats afloat. But like the others, if called upon, she may have also been a formidable enemy. Many Russian trawlers were conceived by naval architects and built under typical Soviet secrecy to the highest specification. They were massively powerful and tough, the heavy steel plating welded around their ribs built to withstand up to fifty millimetre calibre machine gun fire. And many had cannon and machine gun mounts on their bows. Like the ship we were on that evening, the sonar and radar equipment on the bridges was amongst the most sophisticated in the world. Some were even thought to have had a system of nuclear wash down capability as well – for good measure.

They were the USSR's secret navy, in addition to the one we all knew about. Quickly convertible to military use, these Jeckyl and Hyde ships of the high seas could fish, fight, feed and defend.

Intelligence gathering was also par for the course.

I followed the commissar's broad back into the belly of the ship. Behind me, the mezzanine steps clattered with the sound of Laurie and Chubb's boots. The corridor we'd dropped down into ran the centre of the ship and was dimly lit with bulkhead lights. It pulsated in time with the thud of a generator hidden somewhere below. Above the thumping came a noise like a cheap radio, turned up too loud, punctuated with marching music, echoing from somewhere ahead, and it was getting louder as we clanged along.

"Someones having a party." Chubb grinned round at me.

"Aye." I pulled a face. "More than we are." The case of beer was making my fingers ache.

A few more paces and we identified the source of the noise. It was coming from behind a wide door, its fingerplate grimy with use. As we drew level, the door opened. The noise increased tenfold and a man fell out into the corridor blinking with the light. I sidestepped to avoid him. He stunk of strong Russian tobacco, which wasn't surprising given the clouds of smoke following him from the room.

Inside looked suspiciously to me like the ship's galley, but it was in darkness. The only light came from an ancient 8mm projector. Like a knife it cut across the room through the smoke, playing what looked like an old propaganda newsreel onto a screen. Heavy vehicles towed rockets, flanked by marching troops, and a Russian voice-over sounding triumphant rattled from a mono speaker.

Heads began to turn as we watched, faces showing white in the wedge of light thrown from the open door.

"Bloody hell, they know how to live" Chubb said. "Sad bastards."

The big man who had been striding on ahead, keen to get us past, came back, pushed between us, reached in and pulled the door firmly shut.

It was obviously not part of our tour.

A few doors along, he stopped and ushered us into a small cabin. Inside, four steel grey walls, one with portholes painted shut, surrounded a table that nearly filled the floor. We had been led into a tiny wardroom. Like the galley, smoke hung thickly in the stale air. The source of which, a slight man with grey cropped hair, sat behind an ashtray, with a tobacco tin and a packet of roll-up papers. In the centre of the table was a tray with a bottle of pale pink liquor and four upturned glasses.

Leaving us at the door, the big man went over and spoke briefly in a low growl, the little man nodding, tapping the ash from his cigarette. When the big man finished, the little man spoke quietly without looking up, choosing instead to draw the ashtray closer and balance his roll-up in one of the four notches on the rim.

It showed me who was the boss.

Our host turned back to us, forcing a grin.

"Gentlemen, please do not stand by the door. Please come in. Come. Yes." He fussed like 'mine host' ushering us toward the benches.

"Come, you meet my friend, Comrade Chevsky. Please."

We scrambled in clattering our cans on the table, eying the centrepiece of spirit.

"Yataslav," the smaller man smiled, shaking our hands. "Please, you call me Yataslav."

The smooth hands gave the lie to the lumberjack shirt and stubble on his chin, and his English was near perfect.

"You are far from your motherland, my friends," he said casually, making another cigarette whilst smoke still curled from the one in the tin tray.

"We Russians are used to this cold." He studied the rolly, engrossed in his work.

"I wonder what could have brought you here?"

Sure, like I'm going to tell you. "Just a routine call, pal." I pulled out three cans, cracked one open, echoed by Chubb and Church, slid one across to him, and held one out to the big man.

But he shook his head from where he leaned against the porthole.

"We like to keep an eye on our guys at the BAS base." I turned back to the little man. "You know, help with any chores, repairs and the like." It was bollocks but it was all he needed to know. "Pretty boring really." I took a pull at my beer. "Tell you what though man, we're dead keen on your communication equipment."

Laurie nodded agreement. "Aye, you've got some fancy gear upstairs alright."

The little man said nothing in reply, but held up a G.I. Zippo, the flame instantly consuming half an inch of his new roll-up, then breathed out a long stream of smoke towards our host. The big man folded his arms and shifted his feet.

"Our bridge? It's nothing. Just some old fashioned Russian equipment. That's all. We need very little on a simple fishing boat my friends." He cracked his can open, took the glasses from the tray in the centre of the table with one hand, a finger in each, slid them expertly around and poured the pink liquid.

"Drink my friends. Soon we will eat." He raised his glass. "Nostrovia." We threw the spirit back. Fire tore at my throat, dowsed by a long pull of Heineken.

"Is good?" he asked.

"Fucking fire water."

He grinned and slopped out more of the rocket fuel, chinking the neck of the bottle on the rim of each glass as he poured.

A couple of beers later, the steel door opened, and to my surprise two women appeared through the smoke with food on trays.

"Oi, Oi, lads. Floor show's here." It was Chubb, rubbing his hands together.

They took no notice. Un-made-up and wearing men's clothing, they reminded me that we were on board a ship of the Communist Soviet Union. They clattered the trays down in front of us, and the "thanks pet" from me to the blonde (that looked like she might brush up a bit) was totally ignored. They had brought us fried sprats in batter with chunks of bread. OK, it looked a bit oily but smelled good.

Watching the women, expressionless and unsmiling, leave the cabin. I realised that they had come in and left without a glance from our hosts.

The two Soviet men would have known basically what was going on at Leith Harbour. After all, the whole world knew, thanks to the press coverage. But they didn't know about our surveillance post, and tactfully stayed off the subject. They would also know that the coincidence of British Marines just turning up on the island at the same time as Davidoff's illegal landing was a bit remote. Probably as unbelievable as them just happening to need to come to the very same safe harbour as the *Endurance* to take on fresh water.

The Cold War game of covert surveillance and info gathering was, after all, played by both sides. The Soviet Union did not have the monopoly.

I watched them as we talked, the big man with his broken English and the little guy, playing 'Mr Easygoing' with his rolly hanging from his lip. What did their masters back at the Kremlin think about the present situation? And which way would their sympathy lie if the Argies pushed their luck too far? Whatever they thought, we would be unlikely to learn it here. Pushing these thoughts from my mind I downed another glass of pink fire, leant back against the steel cabin wall and joined in the craic.

We finally clattered up the steel staircase and emerged back on deck to the full onslaught of the frozen Antarctic night. Hours before, the hoar-frost had fallen like snow. It stood like needles, covering the ships deck – white like a Christmas card.

The big man had led us up. He stood now by the rail, hand outstretched. He'd been a good host, military training was stamped all over him, the craic had been good humoured and easy. And I guessed he was probably stuck on a tub because he was too old for active service. I shook his great paw.

"Hey. You cold English." He growled. And he was right, after the heat of the cabin, the air was slashing through my jumper like a scalpel.

"Fucking brass monkeys pal." I released his hand and made towards Chubb and Laurie, who were already halfway down the gangplank.

"Wait, my friend."

I stopped. The other two turned to see what was going off. He came closer raising his arms towards his head.

"Here, English." He took hold of his great black hat and lifted it from his head.

"You try this." He held it out to me, grinning. His head was shiny and bald on top with two tufts as black as night above his ears.

"Take it," he ordered, offering it to me. "Come. You try. Real Bearskin, my friend. A Russian hat."

I put it on to humour him, then turned and grinned to show the others. It was still hot from his bald head.

Laughter and, "Fuck me its Kruschev," came from the gangplank.

"Let me see?" the Soviet stood back a little, lips pursed as if undecided. Then he drew in a breath, folded his arms and nodded. "You see, English?" The Cheshire Cat grin reached his eyes. "Even you look good in this hat. You take it my friend." He slapped me on the shoulder like a playful Russian bear. "Who knows," he said "you may need it." Then turned on his heel and descended back down the steps into the warmth of the ship.

In the morning the Storki was gone.

CHAPTER 20

RED ALERT

Twilight of the 31st found us heaving our gear from the tender onto the timber jetty at King Edward Point.

"Well gentlemen. The situation has changed yet again." The skipper had briefed us earlier in the ship's canteen. "The Argentines have put to sea. They say they are on naval exercise." There was a general muttering at the phrase. "It is unclear what they are up to but it appears that they are now somewhere between the mainland and the Falklands."

He cleared his throat. "London are not happy about the way things are shaping up and feel that the situation may worsen. That means, gentlemen, we shall be sailing with all due dispatch." He scanned around the room. "It also means, I'm afraid, that in the interests of safety, this is where we part company." He looked at his watch. "We will be dropping you ashore shortly, under the command of Lieutenant Mills," Mills' piercing eyes drilled us, "and you will be billeted, from now on," the skipper carried on, "in Shackleton House."

Before we left the *Endurance*, Mills had made sure we got our full quota of ammo plus a few extra weapons from the naval armoury. I hauled the ship's 84mm Carl Gustav rocket launcher from the deck of the tender onto the woodwork and placed it amongst the pile of ammo boxes.

"Jesus. We've got enough stuff here to start our own little private war." I watched Jesse heave a ton of kit onto his shoulder and head off for Shackleton House. He could make a mess with this little lot.

We had been out all day, ploughing through ice filled waves, steaming up and down our stretch of coast off Cumberland Bay. The skipper was watching the movements of a new ship which had joined the *Bahia Bueno Suceso* the day after we had done our stint on Jason Peak. She was the *Bahia Paraiso*, an Argentine assault ship, and not welcome.

Flying the pennant of Captain Trombetta the Argie Commodore of the Antarctic, she had once again left Leith harbour to patrol off the coast about fifteen miles out, something she had been doing for several days since her arrival. Call me paranoid, but it seemed to me that she was waiting for company. We hadn't closed on her, just played tag. Our twin Wasps, painted with new olive and grey war-paint since my last wave-hop, were out nearly full time recceing the coast.

But now in the dying light, the choppers were back on board the *Endurance* and disappearing with the sound of her engine. With the twilight had settled a dead calm. We stood up from our work on the little jetty and watched her masthead lights twinkling as she left the bay.

Things weren't going as planned.

I shouldered my stuff and followed Jesse. The path led around the right hand side of the wooden promontory between the BAS white painted sheds and workshops, then up a rise towards the big long shape of Shackleton House. The point was on a spit of land which jutted out into the steeply shelved waters of the cove, while the straight beach on the south, leading round to Hope Point, quickly became shallow, and was filled with kelp and rock. The path ran parallel to the shore. Two thirds of the way to the house, I passed the helipad, which was just a slab of concrete – levelled-up – on the sloping shale. Penguins, watching us, had occupied the few feet between its crumbling mortar and the sea. Opposite was the old gaol. I logged the terrain as I walked, hitched up my pack and pulled up my collar against the growing cold.

Another hundred yards and the path wound to the left before rising again to a level ledge at the foot of the cliffs. In the centre of this plateau, surrounded by scree and a broad tangle of tussock grass, stood the great long railway shed of Shackleton House.

It had become night, the lights from some of the ground floor windows had flickered into life. As I made for the entrance porch, a breeze lifted a thin powdering of snow from its roof, leaving the white dust to float gently down onto the frozen rock beneath.

"First floor, George." Chubb was inside the entrance. He lifted his Bergen, pointing at the stairs. "Most of the boffins are down on the ice." He grinned. "Just find a room, they reckon."

We piled up the stairs. Doors lined the long central corridor. I found a room that wasn't occupied, chucked my sleeping bag on the bed and flopped down. Hands behind my head I eased back on the headboard and clocked the contents around me. Good choice. A NAD amp and sound system sat on the cabinet by the bed. Scanning the cassette albums I found Fleetwood Mac's 'Rumours', decided it would do, put on the headphones, leaned back again and cranked up the volume.

I listened to one side, then caught up with forty-five minutes sleep, before returning to the ground floor, where I found Steve Chubb propping up the bar.

"Room to your liking sir?" he slid a pint of lager towards me along the wet Mahogany.

"Aye, but the Room service is crap." I took a long pull. It was near frozen. "Do 'emselves proud, eh?" I nodded at the large room. It was the first time I had been in.

I panned round. Comfortable seats in the corner to the left of the door, on the far wall a dartboard. A pool table in the middle surrounded by guys holding cues, and tables and chairs sat around the rest of the walls. There was still room for a dance. "Nice place."

"Very. Hate to get the barman angry though."

I raised my eyebrows.

Chubb pointed up. "Seen this little baby?"

A beam ran the length of the bar. It was covered in green PVC cloth like the dash of an old car. A wicked looking ice axe hung dead centre.

"Nice."

Brasso came over. "Seen it then?" He glanced up.

"Aye, you'd have a job to miss it, Brasso lad." I replied. The axe glinted in the light.

"Amundson's axe they reckon." He continued looking up at it.

Chubb pushed his empty glass across to me. "Yeah. Do some serious damage with that my son."

Brasso took his eyes from the weapon, bought a packet of crisps, and wandered back towards the pool table.

Chubby's empty glass stood in front of me so I took the hint that it was my shout and ordered two more beers. While I was 'getting them in' a crowd from the *Endurance* detachment came into the room and leant on the woodwork. While I watched the golden liquid flowing from the chrome tap, their conversation drifted across

"Fucking handy innit?" One of them was saying to his oppos, hands in pockets.

"What?"

"The bleedin' *Endurance* legging it like that. Talk about divide and conquer."

"How d'you make that out?"

"Well think about it. If the buggers really are up to something this time, with the ship gone and the choppers gone with it, there's just twenty two of us to guard the whole fucking island."

"Piece of piss. The island's only a hundred miles long. We'll spread out." Laughter from the other guys. "Anyway, it'll never bloody happen. They haven't got the balls my son."

They carried their drinks across to a table and clattered down.

"Think he's right," Chubby looked up, "about them tarting around again?"

"I bloody hope so. The other guy's got a point. But, if anything does kick off, the *Endurance* is more use to us at sea. Think about it, bottled up here she'd be a sitting duck." I shoved in a palm full of peanuts I'd bought from the bar. "Tell you who else isn't happy Chubby," I screwed up the empty packet, "and that's the boffin boss over there."

I inclined my head towards the two scientists who had just walked across the room to join some guys with worried faces that were sat round a side table. I'd seen the two men before: Steve Martin – the leader of the BAS team and the Magistrate of the island, making him answerable only to Rex Hunt – and a guy called Bob Headland. I'd seen Martin when he had visited the ship, but the other boffin I'd met on the island.

"Looks like their governor's lost a pound and found five bob," Chubb laughed.

I thought about it and guessed maybe it had all happened a bit fast for them. It was probably the first time in the island's history that an armed force had seen the need to garrison, and Steve Martin was probably wondering who was now in charge. I also reasoned that he had a right to look a bit hacked off. His island had been invaded twice. First by Davidoff, spraying lead about, and taking up residence in Leith. Now us lot in his own station. We'd given him thirty minutes notice of our occupation – and it hadn't been a request.

Jesse came over with a couple of empties and joined the queue. The beer wasn't bad. I wondered how long it would last. Back at base we were going for a world record and had downed a year's supply in three months.

CHAPTER 21

A VOICE ACROSS THE OCEAN

I slid off the headphones, shading the glare of the overhead light with my arm. 'Wake up in the morning, see the sunrise', the last track of Fleetwood's 'Rumours', was still banging round in my subconscious. The dial on my watch registered 21.15. The date counter had flipped to 01.04.82 whilst we were still in the bar last night. Nothing had changed – still in limbo. So I dropped my arm and swivelled round, rucking up the Arctic sleeping bag. Time I wandered down, see the rest of the night out with a game of pool and a beer.

The day had broken dull and hazy and for once had decided not to go through four seasons in twelve hours. Apart from a period when the temperature had dropped rapidly, coupled with a strong wind clearing the air to crystal visibility in minutes, the sun briefly hammering the white, mountain walls, it was just another day; though it soon settled back to a dull grey drear.

In the morning, Steve Chubb and I left the building and scrunched across the white dusted scree, running round its long south-facing wall, towards a higher plateau on the east. After five hundred yards, Shackleton's memorial stood in front of us, holding pride of place on the highest piece of ground. A tall white granite cross, concreted into a pile of stones, it faced across Cumberland East Bay towards the Barff Peninsula. We hacked up through the long tussock grass and stood in front of it.

"Bit of a mess." Chubb kicked a piece of broken rock.

"Typical." I scanned around. The scruffy vegetation stopped a few feet from the pile. A rusting pipe, that might once have been a fence post, with a bit of manky cable hanging from it, stood at a crazy angle. Barbed wire caught on the pile of stones. Maybe years ago there had been a fence to keep out the island's Reindeer, but not now. The place was desolate and untended. I turned and faced the icy breeze.

"Bit of a view though, Chubby man." The scene across the bay was breathtaking.

"Lucky bugger then." Chubb grinned.

"He's not up here mind. They buried him in the cemetery below Brown Mountain," I pointed across the bay, "just outside town." With our present height, on a clear day you could have seen the neat line of head stones on the other side of the cove.

An elephant seal, hidden below us at the foot of the ridge, boomed out a warning.

"They reckon he was tough as this granite." I tapped the pile with my foot.

I was taught about Shackleton at school, one of the few lessons I enjoyed, and it had stayed with me.

With the South and North poles already discovered, Shackleton reckoned the last great challenge would be to cross the Antarctic from one side to the other, from the Weddell to the Ross Seas. But he didn't get far. His ship, the first *Endurance*, got stuck in the Weddell Sea ice, and he didn't even make the South Pole. It was a failure. He was doomed to drift with the pack-ice for nine months before the ship finally sank. I guess many would have given in to their fate, but Shackleton turned the disaster into his greatest success. When the flow broke enough, he and his crew managed to sail the three ship's whalers through the ice to Elephant Island. From there he took five men and set sail for the nearest inhabited island, South Georgia, a journey of eight hundred miles.

The elephant seal on the beach below us broke into my thoughts with another warning roar. I could hear it grunting as it shifted its weight on the shale.

"Noisy bastard." Chubby tossed a piece of shale into the long grasses.

Shackleton and his men spent fifteen days at sea in the worst conditions on earth, fighting the 22 foot cockleshell boat through mountainous seas. Cold, and constantly wet, they endlessly fought to break the tiny boat free of the frozen sea spray that coated every inch in its deadly grip. When they eventually reached land, they had to stand off for another two days in storm conditions. Their landfall was on the south shore. The only habitable space on South Georgia is on the north face. They had no choice now but to cross the island – a feat never before attempted by man.

Shackleton led the team across, climbing snow-covered mountains and glaciers, to a height of three thousand feet. They did not take a tent, so they could rest only for short periods. If they stopped too long in their exhausted state and fell asleep in the snow, they would have frozen to death. They marched for thirty-six hours and covered forty miles, finally finding the whaling station at Stromness on the other side of the mountains, and help.

By the time Shackleton returned to Elephant Island to rescue his crew, two years had passed since the start of their voyage. Every man survived, and, against all odds, Shackleton got them all home.

A breeze blew up, rustling the tall grasses. I looked down the slope towards the green walled and red roofed bulk of the BAS station. The great Norwegian explorer Amundson, first man to reach the South Pole, had been here too, his ice axe proof of that, hanging above the bar. It occurred to me that Sir Ernest Shackleton was in good company.

We kicked around the site a bit longer, then retraced our steps to the house.

Darkness had fallen, with its usual pitch-black canopy, filled with a million twinkling stars, heralding the start to another sub zero Antarctic night. My watch had registered 21.20 when I returned to the ground floor and pushed through the bar doors, into tobacco smoke and the hum of voices.

The beer was holding out well, as was the bird behind the peanut card. Two more bags, I reckoned, and we'd be down to her tits. I shoved in another palm full and watched the *Endurance* guy miss his ball.

"Bollocks." He said.

"Nice shot." Steve Chubb did his laugh. We were playing in pairs and I had time to kill – two more before my turn – so I picked up the little cube of blue chalk and idly twisted it on my cue. One of the BAS guys walked past, and I only half noticed him. After a day outside in the cold, the warmth, and the chatter, were sweeping over me in waves. He pushed his way between the busy tables until he finally reached the big radio, half hidden by its circle of armchairs by the side wall, and switched it on.

Whines and crackles joined the hum of voices. I put down the blue cube of chalk and watched him carefully searching the airwaves – probably the only contact the BAS team had with the outside world, but I paid little attention to what he was doing.

Derisory laughter had broken out from the small crowd on the other side of the hall. Another arrow had missed the cork. It hung out of the halo of pockmarks surrounding the board for a second, then dropped onto the floor below.

The whining crackled in my ears, then blurred into an amplified voice, jacking up the noise in the room. I looked at my watch. It was almost 23.30. He was probably looking for the World Service.

The clock above the scrum at the bar agreed with my Rolex. I watched it ticking, its clear face showing the second hand climbing by degrees slowly towards its zenith. Something about its hesitant kick took my mind back to the tiny creatures I'd seen just a few hours before.

Captured and held prisoner in Bob Headland's laboratory just along the corridor, minute insects that live in the Antarctic's permafrost were being studied for their incredible ability to survive. The scientist had shown me some that he had attached to minute electrodes. They could survive sustained temperatures of sixty degrees below, surviving through their own unique anti-freeze. Not dead, but recording no discernible signs of life, they were just waiting for the boffins to raise the temperature in their prison of ice and they would miraculously twitch back into life.

The man by the radio turned up the volume, jolting me back to the present. He had found the wavelength that he had been searching for, the whines and crackles had stopped and a voice boomed out across the room. It was one a lot of us recognised and heads turned from the bar towards it. It was Rex Hunt. There came a seconds silence, and the room fell quiet. The voice spoke clearly and calmly from the mono speaker behind the veneered lattice.

It was surreal. Most of us gathered in a mob around the set. The governor was sending out a message from the Capital Radio Station, a stones-throw from Government House, for anyone who cared to listen.

Eight hundred miles to our north-west, the Argentine naval exercise, as predicted, had become an armada. It had finally arrived at the Falklands and was standing twenty miles off the coast of Port Stanley. The storm clouds were ready to break. Rex Hunt was preparing the island and her dependencies for the "probability of an imminent invasion."

The South Atlantic War was about to begin.

When our friend left the airwaves, the silence in the room was absolute – for a nanosecond – before bursting into a sea of voices.

"What the hells going on Steve?" The survey team were near the set quizzing their leader.

"Did you know about this?"

"Have they been coming through on the VHF radio and warning you about this, man?"

"Why the bloody hell weren't we informed?!"

"Good God. Should have put two and two together. Place full of ruddy Commandos."

So, none of them were bloody Einstein then.

I joined our lot at the bar.

"Think the bastards'll really do it this time George?" Brasso pulled at his shirt collar.

"Reckon so." I looked across at Mills talking earnestly with Pete Leach. "You know yourself it's been building for months, man."

"Wouldn't have gone on the bleeding radio otherwise, would he?" Chubb butted in.

"Aye, fucking encrypto's will be red hot my son." I grabbed a stool. "Christ knows if they'll be coming here, mind."

"That's a point," Jesse joined in. "Might not need to. It's a classic case of divide and conquer, right?"

"See what you mean," I put in. "The bastards send Davidoff down here as a fucking decoy." He nodded. "We chase down after him."

"And they are six nil up before the game has even started." Chubb jumped in.

"Brilliant. They've split us up good and proper, haven't they."

"Aye, Chubby, man. Think about it." I broke back in with my train of thought. "They've got us lot out of the way, and the *Endurance*. That's twenty two Marines, a bloody great pile of assault weapons and two choppers. Great." I grabbed my glass from the bar and threw back the half inch of beer. "Tell you what. If they planned it to happen, then it's fucking faultless."

Eight hundred miles of ocean separated us from our friends. Marooned on a frozen rock, and powerless to help them. A fucking balls up. We might as well have been on the moon.

We drew up tables and sat closer to the radio. The broadcast had been replaced by music, followed by the calm measured tones of Pat Watts, Falkland Island DJ, and presenter. Surreal. I pictured him in his little bungalow, wired for sound, big black head phones, leaning over the mic.

After several tracks, his friendly reassuring voice, perfect for birthdays and anniversaries, was asking the civil population to stay indoors. Then a few more discs, and he was mobilising the civil defence. I guess he was in constant touch with Hunt, playing the governor's bizarre requests.

The initial cacophony of sound in the bar faded as we waited. The first tortuous seconds stretched into minutes and the noise of voices retreated like an ebbing tide. The unanswerable questions in our minds were reduced to silence. Our ears waited for every message and an intense calm slowly descended upon the room like a heavy curtain. Now and then, as the quarters stretched into hours, a chair would scrape and fall back, and I'd look away from the set to clock another back disappearing through the swing doors. Someone else had left.

The coffee was keeping me going. I hung on every word, which in truth wasn't much. Nothing much had happened yet.

The detachment from the *Endurance* were pig sick too.

"So where the hell is she then?" One of the guys on the next table had spat, hours earlier.

"Don't have a go at me old son." His oppo sounded just as frustrated.

"Listen, stands to reason, they don't call her the bloody plum for nothing pal. She's visible for bleeding miles, right. Don't matter how brave she is, she can't take on a full blown bleeding warship, even if it is a bloody Argy."

"Yea he's right, mush. She can either push on to the Falklands, find a safe place to keep out of the way – Maybe Cumberland Bay East." Another guy had joined in, doing a thumb over his shoulder, "or, she can go like a bat out of hell for South Africa."

He'd summed it up well. She was best off out of it.

They'd left a while ago, their empty glasses were still on the table.

This left just a few of us now, waiting, with 'Strangers in the night' pumping from the box by the wall.

Two more tracks, and the music stopped with a click. I let my front chair legs fall silently to the carpet. Every mans head turned towards the radio. Something was happening. The unmistakeable voice of The Governor of The Falkland Islands and Her Dependencies, Rex Hunt, had returned, and vibrated through the speaker.

Concise and unruffled, his message hammered across eight hundred miles of ocean. The waiting was over. He was declaring a formal state of emergency.

So they'd done it.

His understated words had told us what we needed to know. That Argentine Forces had landed, with aggression, on British soil.

I pushed back my chair, picked up my mug and crossed the room for more coffee. Anxious faces met my eyes. The smoke in the room made them smart and sting, like they were filled with grit. I didn't need the caffeine but I took a swig anyway, swallowing fast. It was stale and tasted like shit. My watch registered 04.25 – the numbers sliced into my memory like a white hot brand. No point in sleep now. I sleeved the moisture off the triple-glazed window and peered out into the Arctic night.

One hour. One hour to 'stand-to', and the near frozen rain was lashing down.

CHAPTER 22

FORCE 11

"Shit. Hear that?" Chubb spat the words. Sounds of warfare had replaced the music and were now spewing out across the airwaves.

I was finding it hard to focus. I rubbed my eyes – the bad dream was getting worse. Hunt was now holed up in Government House and giving a sporadic commentary on the battle that was literally raging around him. My ears picked up cracks from SLRs and sustained bursts of automatic gunfire behind his words.

"Mad bastard's probably got the mic under his desk!" a bearded scientist from the survey team shouted across from his position by the set.

He looked bleary-eyed and about all in.

We hadn't time to hear any more – just pushed through the door to hear the latest on our way outside. A noise that sounded like a grenade going off inside the governor's building rang out from the speaker as the doors slapped shut behind me.

Brasso was in the corridor hauling on his Arctic windproof. "Anything new?" His eyes were a mix of anger and uncertainty.

"Same shit." I brushed past. "Nothing we can do about it my son."

The battle for the Falklands had started shortly after Hunt's announcement. He'd been back on the air from 6.25 a.m., broadcasting from his office. He had given us a running commentary of events, at least as much as he could tell from his position. We had heard our outnumbered and out-gunned friends, having fallen back to defend Government House, now fighting for their lives. It was like a living nightmare. I didn't want to hear any more; maybe the outside world would clear my head.

I grabbed the big stainless latch and bent out of Shackleton House into the Antarctic weather front. It hit me like a solid sheet of water. Breath catching in my throat, I coughed and spat phlegm with its breathless onslaught. Anything was better than that damned room. The radio had started to look like a coffin. I needed to know what was going down but would have gladly thrown the thing across the room for telling me.

I snatched a spade from the pile and half-walked half-swam through the onslaught towards the centre ground between the porch and the edge of our plateau. I clocked the terrain – near perfect. Jesse and Brum appeared like shadows out of the squall. This was where we would dig.

"Good spot!" Jesse shouted into the near gale. Rain hammered down his spade handle and ran off the end like a shower head.

"Aye, couldn't be better man." The weariness had dropped off me and it felt good to be doing something I knew.

"Echelon?" He tried to raise his eyebrows in the squall then resorted to running the blade along the saturated hillocks of grass in an arrowhead.

"Straight down," I scowled, pointing a finger.

He grinned. "Yep. If they're coming from anywhere it'll be straight up. Can't see 'em chancing the shore."

"Too much shit," I agreed. "If they use assault craft the props will snag in the kelp. The rocks look a bastard too. Can't see 'em chancing it. Only other way in is Hope Point, just below the cross." I pointed a saturated arm to the high ridge at the end of the house. "Chubb and Parsons have got it covered." Their position overlooked a good landing ground amongst the elephant seals just below the monument.

"Shit." Jesse looked up. "If they go down we're bolloxed." He hacked his blade deep into the peat between the clumps of grass. Brasso appeared through the horizontal sleet and took a pickaxe to the north corner. Jesse didn't need to tell me what would happen. If a force put in and overran Chubby's Bren gun position, they would come in from behind and above us. We'd be dead meat.

I squinted into the stinging rain, down the long line of beach that our L-shaped trench would overlook. The helipad was clear in our sights, no more than 130 yards below us. Then a good 400 yards of beach with no cover, unless you counted the penguins. We also commanded a straight view directly down the rough track between the sheds and bungalows. I spat salt and tried to wipe it from my eyes with near frozen fingers. The pity was that our sightlines were cut off a few feet from the end. Just a few rusting huts stood between our position and a clear line of fire, through to the deep water jetty at the very tip of the point.

If they came for us, this was our killing ground.

Two survey team guys came across with spades and we slowly began to make a dent. The peat was a bitch to dig though; once past the tough grass roots it had become easier but the deeper we dug the more the trench filled with near frozen water.

One degree less and the ground would once again freeze back to its armour plating of ice.

I looked up, ran my fingers round my roll-over and straightened. Despite the frozen rain, I could still feel a trickle of sweat on my back. I scanned the narrow waist of the plateau across to the left of me, after a hundred yards or so it bulged out again, maybe two three times the size of my ridge. It was a hive of activity with bodies digging like us. Visibility was down to zilch, though I could just make out six more trenches.

Dark shapes of people began to peel off, heading back towards the house. I checked my watch – nearly time they were gone, like us their BAS guys were on the move. They were moving out at nine.

"Best off out of it." Jock Hunter stood next to me, leaning on his spade, watching their retreating backs. "Guess Mills thinks the church is the safest place for 'em."

I pictured the small white timber building on its patch of grass beneath Mount Hodges where the thirteen men would hole up just in case. Mills had told them to take enough food, drink and bedding to see them through. If it kicked off I guess a holy place, even if it was only a whalers' chapel, might give them some kind of sanctity. The Argies are superstitious buggers. Sure as hell though, the walls wouldn't be stopping any bullets.

Our kit was already there. We'd packed our Bergens with our spare clothing rations and sleeping bags earlier and heaved them up onto the BAS tractor and trailer.

The wind blasted the side of my face. The black bearskin hat was made for these conditions and maybe I should have heeded the Russian Commissar's warning. But it was stuffed in my kit, probably under a pile of other gear, somewhere in the whaler's church. I pushed it from my mind, climbed back down into the watery trench and sunk my blade deep into the stinking peat.

"Stand to. Stand to!" rang out from somewhere to my right. It was Sergeant Major Pete Leach.

Bodies threw themselves down. I was outside the water-filled hole and dropped prone, belly down, into the long saturated grass.

Jock was nearest the edge of the plateau and I could see his face through a valley in the clumps. Keeping his head low, he glanced back at me, rain hammering into his eyes, and pointed seawards. I crawled forward, my body hugging the ground, parted the grass on the edge of the ridge and peered directly into the squall.

Across the bay a big ship had entered our waters. It looked like the *Bahia Paraiso* – the shape was right but I couldn't be sure. If it was, it was Trombetta, poking around. Maybe he wanted to clock the *Endurance* again but this time he was out of luck. He'd see nothing and no one. He'd find out we were still here when we let him know.

Maybe a quarter of an hour ticked by. I watched her fade in and out of the mist.

"She's going," Jock hissed.

He was right. Her shape changed, then changed again, blurring in and out of the murk as she turned. Through the downpour I watched her slowly leave the bay. In minutes, my eyes couldn't make her grey bulk out from the driving water. Everything was a blur. The sky was now joined to the sea and there was no horizon. It had to be force ten now, going on eleven. My ears filled with rain and the howling roar of the wind. My lower body was soaked and I was shaking uncontrollably with the cold. I gave it another minute, shook the streaming water from my face, found my spade where I'd dropped it and staggered back through the gale to the muddy trench.

Later, much later, I threw down my spade, the noise of its fall inaudible through the howling wind, and thrust my frozen hands into my jacket pockets. My palms were split with blisters and stung like hell with the salt carried by the driving rain.

Les Daniels was finally closing in. I had first picked him out in the last semi light of the day, stooping, reeling, crouching into the onslaught on the long stretch of beach. He was now climbing the last thirty feet to our position, loping sideways, checking his footing every few seconds in the tangle of grass. He saw me and grinned.

"Oi, oi, George." He held up the drum like it was the answer to everything.

"Got you a nice little present mate."

"You spoil us." He hadn't wrapped it.

"Here, what about something for me?" Brum climbed out of the hole.

"Learn to bleeding ask nicely, you brummy bugger."

Les was living proof of the chirpy cockney.

He draped the tangle of wires over the parapet. Hanging from the ends was a white plastic light switch. I watched it swing back and forth like a hangman's noose in the gale.

He'd brought us a deadly surprise at the flick of a switch.

CHAPTER 23

THE LAST SUPPER

John Stonestreet, Royal Marine commando and chef, heaved another large tray of steaming food from the kitchen worktop and brought it across to the hatch.

"Keep it coming, my son."

"If he was prettier, I'd marry him."

"Bugger off, we're already engaged," carried across the din of chatter and clashing cutlery. John clanged the steel dishes down on the canteen bar.

"Christ, John. Where the bloody hell did you get this lot?" Chubb asked the question that was on my mind as we stood at the canteen bar.

John wiped the sweat from his forehead with the back of his sleeve. The white Chef's jacket he'd found was splattered with gravy. "Millsie, Steve. Good bloke. Not like some of the dozy Ruperts we've had to nursemaid. 'Raid the freezers' he said. 'If it's our last supper we'll make it a good one'." He grinned. "So wrap your teeth round it my son, there's a pile more in the kitchen."

"Come on mate. We're bleedin starving back 'ere. Hurry up!" sailed above the laughter.

John raised a finger in salute and headed back towards the steel serving dishes.

"Nice one." I grabbed a spoon and dug in, ladling a pile of spuds onto my plate.

Mills was just visible by the opposite wall with Pete Leach. I took my full plate over to our table and watched him above the heads. His cool bright eyes, haloed with dark rings, were slowly scanning round the room. He looked at Pete and said something. Pete's teeth showed white in a grim smile.

Our spare kit was already stashed elsewhere, so if we had to pull out tomorrow, like Napoleon's soldiers, we'd be marching on a full stomach.

The kitchen doors swung outwards and Stonestreet staggered out with his own plate. The far corner cheered him on like he was the cabaret.

I filled my mouth with the hot food, my mind still wrestling with the onslaught of the day's weather. Memories of the hammering rain were washing away and blurring into the welcome racket around me.

When we had first sat down, the storm, which had built up to force eleven, was clearly visible outside the thick glass of the windows. It was hidden by a heavy layer of condensation now, and might have been in another world, its fury rendered invisible, and its howling swamped by our noise.

I tried to focus on the day's events. The image of Daniels and his team striking in and out of the shacks that lined the track and scrabbling around on the shore below us, came and went in my head between the chatter. Then the noise jacked up another notch, as John headed back into the kitchen to organise the pudding.

Across the table Jesse reached past Chubb and hooked in a salt pot.

"The boy's done us proud Steve." he nodded towards John Stonestreet's retreating back.

The reply was mumbled, but I caught the laugh through the clamour. Behind them I clocked the water now streaming down the inside of the windows. Several drips joined on their journey to the sill travelling left then right before disappearing from my view. I took a pull at my glass, carefully replaced it onto the wet ring by my plate, and carried on eating. So, it was my last supper? Then I'd do it justice.

Two hours later after an 'O' group meeting with the boss, Pete Leach, Al Larkin, and Nige Peters, I joined the others at the bar. We'd had sentries out since nightfall doing half hour shifts. It was enough in a force eleven. I'd just passed two on my way down the corridor and I could feel the cold radiating from the poor sods as they pushed past.

"Nothing?" I asked.

It was odds on there wouldn't be. No one in their right mind would launch an attack in this weather.

"Bugger all. And if there is, we'll soon have to send bleeding smoke signals."

I raised my eyebrows.

"Radios are nearly fucked aren't they? It might have helped if some silly sod had checked the batteries."

They'd been watching from Hope Point; the high ground gave the best view over the entrance to the cove. There was no other way in.

In the bar Chubby had lined them up. I grabbed one and looked at the peanut card – maybe I could manage a bag later.

Les Daniels was in the crowd, he reached in and grabbed a beer.

"Cheers mate." He said, then held up the glass and took a swill.

"So where's the power from, Les?" I rested an elbow on the woodwork and hooked a stool in with my boot. Odds on he couldn't have had the switch attached in this rain – the wires would short circuit in seconds.

"No problem mate. Got it well sussed. Found an old arc-welder down in one of the workshops. Big old bastard it is, size of a bleeding chest freezer," he grinned. "We'll be powered up to that in the morning."

"What's on the end of it then?" Holden broke in. Les swigged his beer. Laurie

Church, one of his team that morning, answered for him.

"Glad you asked Brum. It's a double switch my old acker. The one on the left is wired-up down to the beach, case they try and storm us with landing craft. It'll set off a series of homemade mines. We've dug 'em in, planting them every few feet along the shoreline under the stones. Found nearly all the stuff we needed in the old sheds."

Les Daniels put down his empty glass and came back in. "And the other switch, the one on the right, is wired up to a shed on one side of the path and the old bungalow opposite, Quigleys House it's called. Figured we need to take out as many as possible George," he grinned up at me, "so we've stuffed a load of old ammo boxes for you with PE4 and packed a load of gear around it. The usual stuff, you know, nuts, bolts and nails, even found a pile of old harpoon heads."

He looked pleased with that. I pictured him cutting the white oblongs of plastic explosive to size with his penknife then moulding it round the charges like a roll of soft white icing. "Press the switch my old mate," he carried on, "and it'll be bleeding carnage."

I'd seen what Claymores could do: body parts that a surgeon wouldn't recognise, hanging from hedgerows, and knew that it wouldn't be pretty. But, if they attacked, then what would their numbers be? So far we had only seen the two large ships. They were probably carrying scores of American-trained Argentine Marines between them, and the hangers on the *Bahia Paraiso* were probably packed too. After all, reason told us, they weren't there for decoration. We had no idea how many choppers they could be carrying and what kind of destructive firepower they could bring down on us. So if the invasion force were reinforced with more ships and they decided to storm us, we would have to use every dirty trick at our disposal to even the odds.

I would brief my guys in the trench when to use the devices for maximum effect – I'd want every one of the enemy Marines out of the craft and onto the beach before we detonated. Every man we took down would be a bonus and increase our chances of survival.

Explosives expert Daniels' team had also been at work on the quay. Mills had asked Les to do his worst, and he had. Working against the blinding gale, the three men had fought to strap a forty-five gallon drum, filled with petrol then laced round with a necklace of high explosives, underneath the timber boards. Strapped to the device was a large wooden crate, full of six-inch nails and scrap iron for good measure. They had then laid back wires from the booby trap, which would become a fireball when ignited, through the tangle of quayside sheds to the workshop and the big old arc welding machine.

"Be a shame if they don't use the jetty, Les." I looked sideways at him, while waiting for another beer.

"No problem mate. If an Argy ship gets anywhere near it," he pulled a grim smile, "then," he brought his hands together in front of his chest like he was touching the earth and positive leads together on the welder, "Whammo! The fucking jetty goes out to meet it."

CHAPTER 24
COLD STEEL

Later that evening, after a game of pool, I wandered over to the bar. Pete Leach stood with his back against the counter, nursing a mug of coffee. The place was getting quieter. It seemed different; bigger somehow, hollow and emptier. The last bit made sense, because the scientists were holed up in the church. And there were just the twenty-two of us.

The tension of last night was beginning once again to bite. It had been 24 hours now since the invasion. We knew that the Falklands had been overrun, but none of us knew how many of our mates had gone down, nor when the enemy would be gunning for us. There was no point in pretending it wasn't going to happen. It was the waiting that was the bastard – the bastard waiting – it was gnawing at my gut like a hungry rat. I rested an elbow on the counter and found the kick bar with my instep. Around the quietening room some of the guys were sitting silently, not joining in with the others; I guess, like me, they had their own private thoughts.

Our position could have been worse mind, much worse. The weather was our greatest friend, without it we'd never have got dug in. Also, the enemy had to come from the sea, and they would be suicidal to attempt to land in the present weather conditions. It gave us a breathing space. Coupled with that, we were safe-ish here in Shackleton House, the civilians if you like, were our shield. The Argentines had no idea where the survey team were, and an indiscriminate attack by them could end in civvy casualties – the last thing the Junta wanted. They needed the world on their side – to see us as the colonial thieves, and them taking back what they hoped the international community would see as Argentinian by right. No, we were safe in here for now. When they came, it would be in daylight.

Pete Leach placed his coffee mug on the bar.

"That ship today Sarge," I looked round the faces as I spoke. "I take it, it was the *Bahia Paraiso*?"

He folded his arms, "Yeah. That cheeky man Trombetta again George, I'll give him Commodore of the bleeding Atlantic."

"Didn't stay long."

"Long enough." He changed feet on the kick bar, his eyes flicking to Brasso who had left his table. "Wanted to give us a message."

"Yeah?" Brasso walked over looking up.

Leach took his eyes off the room and leaned round on the bar.

"First he tells us that Rex Hunt has surrendered the Falklands and her dependencies, the lying bastard. Falklands yes, but dependencies no. Then, tells us that we will be getting an important message tomorrow. Cocky sod."

I turned towards the silent radio. The red chairs were now empty, but the scientists that usually occupied them hadn't all gone up to the church, there was still one around – their boss, Steve Martin. He wasn't in the big room so I guessed he was still down the track, maybe with Mills. Martin was an expert with the Racal radio in the radio shack. Years of use meant he could fine tune the powerful piece of kit maybe as well as Laurie. We'd be a man less without the help.

I grabbed my coffee off the bar and swirled the brown liquid round. It was warm and sweet.

Martin had another objective for being right there at the sharp end, gathering what information he could, no matter how sketchy: he still had his responsibilities. In fact he was still maybe top man. Well that's what he probably reasoned. He was the island's Magistrate; Hunt's envoy and the Base Commander. So technically he was still in charge.

The guy with the beetles, Bob Headland, had stayed on a bit too. But he was gone now, up at the chapel with the rest of the civvies. I'd seen him earlier through the gale, making his way down the track between the huts, lugging a heavy sack. He'd filled it with documents and encrypto cyphers. It was destined for the deep waters of the cove.

I put down my coffee. The noise in the room was building, some of the guys had moved across for refills and Chubby pointed at my mug, doing the action with his hand, but I shook my head.

"Oi, look out!" was accompanied by a scraping. It came from the other side of Pete Leach. Then Brasso's head appeared above the rest of the guys. I took my heel off the kick bar and stepped away from the woodwork, to see what was going down.

"Go on my son." someone shouted.

The Sergeant Major's brows creased, he moved away like me and looked up, head on one side. Brasso was up on a stool, his face intense, lifting Amundson's ice axe from its fixings above the bar.

"Wahay. It's Excalibur!" Came from the small crowd.

Faces round the room watched. Brasso turned to the audience, held up his trophy, knuckles white, and pulled a grim smile. "Yeahh!" he shouted, and jumped down to the carpet.

"Look out it's the mad axe-man!"

"Geroni-bloody-mo!" An Indian war whoop sliced through the room.

I followed Leach, shouldering through the small crowd.

Brasso, grinning, was slapping the shaft of the wicked looking axe up and down in his left palm.

"All right, you silly sod," Chubb laughed, "so now you got it, what you going to do with it?"

"Do with it? I'll tell you what I'm going to do with it." Brasso stopped slapping the shaft, gripped the axe and held it menacingly over one shoulder. "When I run out of bullets, my son," he brought the axe up in a hacking arc, "the first fucking Argy over my trench will be wearing this in his chest."

The room went very quiet, he wasn't trying to be funny – the only noise came from the howling gale outside, trying to bust in the windows.

The Sergeant Major broke the spell.

"Right lad, that's enough." He stepped into the horseshoe of men. "Come on, jokes over, give it here." He held out a hand like a dinner plate, eyes drilling into Brasso.

A gust slammed into the outer skin of the building with a thump. For a nano second, the room fell dead silent. I looked round the apprehensive faces. Brassos hesitation was momentary, his eyes fell and he held out the weapon.

"It's not a toy, lad." Leach's fingers folded round the steel. "You just leave it here where it belongs."

He turned his back on Brasso's audience, with a barely discernable shake of his head in my direction. His eyes were taking the piss. Brasso was one of my team, one of the NP8901.

"That's just him, Sarge," I nodded not grinning. Brasso was one of the best, a cliché I'd make no excuses for – the reason I'd brought him. When we started to dance he'd be fighting to win. "High spirits, that's all." I picked up my mug and swilled round the cold liquid. The caffeine left a stain an inch from the bottom. I was sick of the stuff.

Ten minutes ticked by, some of the guys at the bar drifted back to their tables, Brasso left the room, another game of pool started and the excitement gradually subsided back into a low hum of voices. A couple of the guys clattered their chairs back and headed for the door, one checking his watch. I automatically turned my wrist and clocked mine, yeah, ten to. I watched them leave. The lashing rain hammering at the thick outer sheets of the treble layers of glass told its own story. The next two poor sods were about to take their turn outside in the freezing rain.

The doors had slapped mockingly behind them, then, minutes later, dragged me back from my thoughts when they flew open again, smashing loudly against the walls on either side.

Brasso was back.

The doors rattled and banged behind him, flying backwards into the corridor, then back again into the bar like they belonged in a saloon in Dodge City. All heads flew round to face him. He stood, framed by the white paintwork, legs wide, eyes flashing round the room. What the hell had he got now?

Cradled in his arms was the hasp of another axe, glinting red like a ribbon of blood across his chest. It was huge, the flat chromium head the size of a spade caught in the light and flashed lightening around the room. It was one of the heavy British fire axes kept behind glass in the main corridor, like something you'd expect to see on a medieval battlefield, nothing subtle about it. Amundsen's ice axe was delicate in comparison.

"Yesss." Brasso shouted and held it up, arms straight above his head. "This... is the baby. You'll not take this one off me!"

There was a moment's absolute silence. He dropped the axe back down, shook it whooping like a Red Indian, and disappeared back out into the corridor. The room erupted. My ears filled with war-whoops, shouts and laughter. The tension broke, pouring out like the cork had finally budged from a bottle. It was the best entertainment we could have had. Smiling faces crowded round the bar.

"The boy's finally fucking flipped."

"Never mind him, what about the poor bleeding Argies?"

Pete Leach shook his head at me. "Right, that's it then George. Time I closed the bar. I said we'd only have a couple." He looked at his watch and made towards the hatch.

I couldn't argue with that. He'd made it clear that the bar would be shutting early, but I didn't want him thinking that Brasso was pissed.

"Shit Sarge, don't get the wrong impression, man. Brasso's not drunk." It was my turn to wag my head. "We don't let him drink. He's bad enough stone-cold sober."

Chubb, standing at my left shoulder, waiting for a refill, laughed horribly.

"Nah, he's right sarge. That's just Brasso. He's normally mental."

CHAPTER 25

ENTER THE PREDATOR

Next morning found me outside Shackleton House. I could see Mills down the track, walking between the huts with the Base Commander. Steam was rising from the flat wet shale at my feet, and the outer walls of the house were radiating heat from the risen winter sun. I pulled at the top button of my windproof.

Nirvana was back.

Not a breath of wind touched the tussock stalks around us or the waters of the bay below, where its blue surface appeared so calm that it might have been a sheet of mirrored glass.

The raging of the night had cleansed everything – not just the rocks of the shoreline, or the virgin white peaks above us, but the very air of the place. The gale had removed and swept away with it even the miniscule particles that had hung suspended in the Antarctic ether, leaving the ozone so clear it was like a skin had been peeled from my eyes.

The effect conjured a powerful madness. I could feel its persuasive clutch – the reason why men had been drawn back, time and time again, for just one more shot of a region so contrary it could thrill one moment and kill the next, like junkies on a fix.

But, for us, the odds had now stacked even higher. The violence that stalked us would not be coming from the elements, but by an overwhelming enemy. If we were meant to perish, this place was better than most. Who knows, maybe South Georgia would be a good place to die.

Behind me the porch door slapped shut. Boots scrunched on the loose ground. I tugged at the first button, opened my collar and looked round, it was Chubb and Brum.

"They're here then?" Brum scuffed the shale and thrust his hands into his pockets.

"Aye, so I hear." I watched Mills and Martin disappear into the radio hut. "It's as well we got McCallion back with us, mind."

"Fair point," Chubb grinned, his scar joining the lines of his smile, "always good to know your enemy's strength, but I'm not sure it'll help much in this case, Tirpitz old son."

"When did she arrive, anyway?" Brum kicked at the shale.

"5.30-ish." I pushed my beret back. "Nige radioed in from the OP apparently. That's why Leach went to get 'em back." I scanned the empty bay. "Perfect weather for the bastards."

Chubb and Brum's eyes lifted towards the horizon.

Paddy McCallion was one of the guys who had gone up to the OP with Nige Peters. They were closer to Leith than we had been – watching from the Bussen Peninsula. Paddy was an expert on ships. He'd worked at Harland and Wolf before joining up, maybe that's what gave him a taste for it. He collected data on war ships like some people collected stamps. He could rhyme it off verbatim.

At 05.30 hours he had watched a new arrival power sleekly into harbour. His first take was immediately radioed back, but Mills needed first-hand knowledge, and the team back, pronto.

The only way to get them back had been by sea. It was easy when we had the air power, but a fifteen minute wave hop by chopper was now a two and a half hour trip by boat, and dangerous as hell.

There was only one craft really suitable for the job, especially if the weather changed, and that was the BAS launch. After some heated words with the base commander, Leach had commandeered the vessel from its berth alongside the mined jetty and set off at 06.30 hours. Tethered behind him had bobbed our Gemini assault craft – fast and highly manoeuvrable, if the launch bought one they could try and make a dash for it in the inflatable.

I had watched Leach head off, the clear sunlight reflecting from the bow wave and glinting against the dark blue hull. A tough heavy little craft, the deep steady beat of its inboard engine drifting up from the bay, with a brave pit bull of a man, rock solid behind the wheel.

He knew that he had six miles of open sea to cross each way to bring the men home. He also knew that, if he was spotted by one of the frequently traversing enemy helicopters, he would be unlikely to return.

The report they brought the lieutenant back made for bad listening. But by 0900 hours he at least knew the strength of the latest enemy arrival. Taking on fuel from the *Bahia Paraiso* was the French-built Guerrico. Only a few years old, she was the latest in small powerful frigate weaponry, a warship of the highest calibre.

At over 260 feet long and weighing in at around 1,200 tons, she carried a 100mm semi automatic gun on the forecastle, a pair of 40mms astern (similar to a Bofors). Twin MM38 Exocet rocket launchers were aft, with a crew of around eighty, plus whatever compliment of Marines she had brought. Her sleek, ally superstructure meant that she could shift a bit too, with twin diesel engines capable of powering her along at a mean 24 knots.

The upside was that she was, so far, the only reinforcement for the scores of

Argentine Marines already ashore at Leith, or on board the *Bahia Paraiso*. This was small comfort but better than nothing.

"Come on then, you ugly sod" Chubby broke into my thoughts. He pointed along the track towards the huts, "Boss wants us."

Mills was waving us down.

We trudged down the track, rounded the last shed to find Leach standing on the jetty above the laced petrol drum. We had all been called down.

"Right you horrible lot. God knows why, but the OC wants us all in a photo."

"I haven't done me make up Sarge."

"Shit in it, Royal."

We shuffled into a line.

"Christ, George, whatever you do don't bleeding smile." Chubb was the other side of Paddy. "You look like you're constipated."

"Here, you know why Chubb is so bleeding ugly?" I rested my SLR in the crux of my left arm.

"Why would that be, then." Paddy faced the front and adjusted his beret.

"Caught fire. Lucky for him his mates were about. Yep. Put him out with cricket bats."

Mills tossed his Olympus M10 to Steve Martin, shouldered his sub machine gun, and joined our row at the back. It wasn't the occasion for saying cheese. The shutter opened and closed with a zip, Martin dropped the camera down and let it rest on its straps.

We dispersed and trudged back up the rough shale track between the sheds. The penguins had reappeared on the upper beach and a solitary elephant seal, its huge trunk nose vibrating with indignation, bellowed at us from the water line as we passed.

Back up on the ridge, we resumed tidying the spoil around the trench. Brum reaching down and up, bailing the water that was still seeping in from the peat walls; Jesse, busy with boxes of ammo, laying out belts of tracer for the GPMG.

I watched Chubb and Steve Parsons' backs disappear over the rise towards the cross.

It was the classic calm. But mercifully short.

My ears had picked up the faint unmistakeable sound of rotors, jerking me round, eyes searching the sky in the direction of the noise. I didn't have far to look. Across the bay hovered the menacing silhouette of an Argentine Allouette helicopter.

"Take cover!"

Heads disappeared below parapets. The door flew open into Shackleton House. Following other guys, I dashed towards it.

Inside, we stood panting behind the glass entrance doors.

"Reckon they saw us?" Brasso hissed.

"Nah. Too far away my son."

Pete, standing on the other side of the entrance lobby, nodded agreement.

Through the window, I watched the helicopter flying just above the line of Brown Mountain Ridge maybe 4,000 yards away.

Pete slung his L42 sniper's rifle, speckled with its characteristic stamps and punch marks, across his shoulder and clattered up the stairs.

Slowly, the machine turned as though satisfied with its reconnaissance on the other side of the bay and drew nearer. The whump, whump of its rotors came and went as it traversed Cumberland Bay East, then began its run closer to our camouflaged positions.

Nervously, the French machine twitched about the sky probing around Grytviken Town, then swept past King Edward Point. Hidden by the sheds from our view for a moment it, then swept low and fast over the kelp beds towards Chubb's position by the monument. We lost all sight and sound of the big machine as it banked low over the ridge.

Silence fell like a blanket.

The machine might never have been there. Then, suddenly, came the whump whump whump of the rotors hammering the air as he rose again. Now you see me, now you don't. The bastard knew his game. The machine came back into view, rising up from behind the ridge further out near Hope Point, headed out, nose down, towards deep water, dipped to port, tacked north and hit the pedal.

I watched until he was completely out of sight, then breathed out.

"Ship's back George." Brasso adjusted something in his belt beneath his windproof. It made a metallic clunk as he leant against the door.

"Aye." He was right, Trombetta was back, maybe as much as 5,000 yards out where he'd just rounded into the bay. Another chopper was buzzing round the big ship like a gnat. "I've got a feeling this is it, pal." I rested my SLR on my forearm and clunked down the heavy door catch. "Still, they'll not see us from that distance. Time you got in the trench, son."

The low sun was still casting its oblique shadow across the front of the house. We left the porch and stood to the side in the darkness near the north-west corner. Listening. Watching. Waiting. No Argentine reconnaissance. It had to be safe now to head for our positions.

Brasso and Brum stepped out. Then from above us came a thump and a curse. And a nanno second later a heavy sheet of glass missed Brasso's head by inches, exploding at his feet into a hundred deadly shards.

"What the fuck!"

We stepped back, crouching low into the shadow, and looked up.

Above us, a head leaned out from the glassless frame. It was Pete Leach. He'd heard the expletive, I saw his eyes take in the scene, splinters of glass littering the path.

"Shit sarge, you nearly poxing killed us." Brasso wasn't happy.

"Sorry." The broad face grinned wickedly and disappeared from view. The Sergeant Major had decided that if he needed to take up a position on the first floor of the house, then he wouldn't be needing the glass to spoil his view.

Staying low, we padded from the shale path onto the silent tussock grass, back to our positions. The sound of furniture being moved around on the first floor of Shackleton House faded to nothing as we neared the edge of the ridge.

Brasso and Brum disappeared below the parapet of the trench, joining Jesse James. I settled low between the tall grasses a few feet from Jock.
Everyone had gone to ground.

We'd play it by ear now, literally. Every pack was down. The batteries had finally run out. We had no comms between my position, Chubb and Parsons' Bren Gun trench on the ridge by the memorial, or the other five trenches on the plateau on the other side of the track.

Command now would be word of mouth. It was a pisser.

I threaded the barrel of my SLR through the still grasses, the familiar wooden stock warm in my left palm, and squinted through the sights at the empty horizon.

The silence thumped in my ears. No, wait. My pulse had given way to another sound. There. It came again. Not a chopper. Heavier... getting louder. A deeper tone, throbbing, coming from the sea.

But apart from The *Bahia Paraiso*, which was way out, the sea was empty.
Then it came. The bayonet-sharp bow of the Guerrico, emerging from behind the cathedral cliff face of Hope Point, a lazy wave curling along her sleek grey plating, slicing like a knife into King Edward Bay.

"Shit. That's no fucking landing craft." Brasso's voice sounded through the stems.

The noise of her diesels grew louder with the advance of each foot of her sleek hull.

She came on, close into the rocks.

The big gun punched into view, barrel swinging round lowering its grey muzzle. Searching.

"Leave it." I flattened lower into the wet ground.

Bridge, superstructure, funnel belching grey smoke, its noise now resonating, bouncing off the mountain walls. Twin Exocet rocket launchers amidships. Then the superstructure curved down and the long sleek stern slid out from behind the rocks. She was alongside and slipping past.

"Hold fire!" I inched round, the glint of my gun sights following her progress.

Men were running along her deck – four pale blue shirts and bright orange Mae Wests, scampering to man the stern mounted Bofors.

She powered on towards Grytviken, becoming obscured by the sheds on the Point. Her bow wave swelled against the shore. She trailed a cloak of thin smoke behind her. My saliva filled with its acrid taste; I spat phlegm into the grass.

Another thousand yards and she was nearing the derelict harbour, then turned in a graceful arc, and began trailing her petticoats back. She returned past the sheds once again, coming into full view, the same distance from shore, close in and curious, like a hunter looking for prey. Her forward gun was raising, lowering and traversing the shoreline, her stern Bofors swinging from side to side, the crew twitchy, tight in behind their armour shield, looking for signs of movement. She dearly wanted to know where we were, or, more like it, if we were even here.

We hugged the ground, stayed low and watched her pass. She left the cove as she had entered, disappearing yard by yard behind the rocks of Hope Point.

CHAPTER 26

FIREFIGHT

The steady throb of the war ship diminished, muffled by the cliff face, her foaming wake crashing against the rock. Then another sound began to penetrate, drumming in and out of earshot with menacing familiarity. I scanned urgently. Where? A shout rang out from the other plateau.

I turned my head towards the sheds. But there was nothing.

Then it came again, closer, louder. Rotors flashed above a rusting tin roof, bobbing up, then disappearing behind the buildings, it was an Alouette sweeping in low and fast, just feet above the water. After only seconds out of view, she reappeared, rising up, just a glimpse of rotors between the jumble of tin, going like a bat out of hell towards Grytviken. Bodies appeared, flitting between the tin huts by the jetty. The Alouette's tail dropped from view behind the distant town rooftops.

She'd done her job. There would be six enemy below us, amongst the sheds, maximum. OK, they still had no idea of our positions. But now they were coming – in force.

A few seconds passed and my eyes picked up their reinforcements. A flash of blades in the sunshine gave the big machine away as she bobbed down between the mountain valleys then dropped low over the little church, before disappearing into our blind spot behind the sheds of the Point. Half a minute's silence and she reappeared, loud and aggressive, full frontal, then swept round the huts over the jetty and hovered, thirty-feet up, above the helipad. Her blades slammed the air, smashing down onto the sparse vegetation below. She was a troop carrier: sixteen Marines plus air crew – and worse, a gunship! A belt-fed heavy machine gun swung from the open side door, panning round menacingly. A helmeted head peered along the sights. Behind the gunner, pale faces of Marines crammed the fuselage. But what the hell was the pilot doing? The front came up and yawed like he was out on a day trip.

It was a gift.

If we allowed this machine to put down we had big trouble.

She was less than a hundred yards from Al Larkin's position, side on and asking for it.

"HIT IT!" Mills bellowed.

Larkin's gun barked twice. His 7.62s ripped through the Argentine gunner, throwing him back inside like a rag doll.

The fuse was lit. A cacophony of gunfire rent the air. Everyone opened up, filling the inside of the fuselage with hot lead.

The pilot kicked the rudder, hauled the big machine round towards Brown ridge and hit the pedal. She tilted and banked away. Sitting on the right, probably with an armoured seat back, he'd be furthest away from the hail of bullets.

Up on one knee in the wet grass, I took careful aim. The SLR kicked viciously into my shoulder, sending twenty rounds through the gaping doorway into the fuselage.

My adrenalin valve had opened wide, set itself on overtime, whacking neat fluid into my senses. Everything slammed into crystal-clear slow motion, like an action replay – every pull of the trigger a deliberate act.

The racket of automatic fire split the air asunder, punctuated by steel hammering through the thin body of the trapped machine, drumming like hail on a tin roof as bullets pierced and left, over the sound of our onslaught.

The gunship writhed in the sky, obscuring the doorway from my sights. Hundreds of rounds in a few short seconds had pumped into the butcher's shop that had once been a cabin. I turned my attention to the flailing rotors and sent twenty rounds into the engine cowling beneath. Bits of ally and steel rained down from her into the water beneath.

Brum's GPMG, fed feverishly by Brasso, barked and jumped on its bi-pod, sending arcs of lazy tracer across the water. The white-hot stars joined Chubb and Parson's Light Machine Gun tracer, hammering through the ether from my left, and converged, as one, on the retreating machine, like deadly ribbons on a maypole.

Black smoke began to conceal our target.

"We got the bastard, Brum!" Brasso yelled through the din – between them they were pumping out a cyclic rate of 950 rounds a minute – then blew on his burnt fingers and linked another flailing ammunition clip.

The fizz and roar of a 66mm rocket joined the barrage, snaked across the widening gap, brushed the underside of the stricken gunship's fuselage then fell somewhere beyond, exploding in a pillar of white spray.

She veered and wobbled just above the icy water, acrid smoke making patterns in the clear blue sky. I lowered my smoking barrel, released my finger from the warm trigger, slammed in another clip, and watched her crash on the other side of the bay like a broken toy.

Burnt oil and powder tasted strong in the warm air. I ran a finger under my beret and wiped the sweat with the back of my hand.

The 'day tripper' pilot had made the far bank, maybe 1,000 yards away, before losing control and falling out of the air. The Puma lay on her side, rotors crushed with the impact, a crippled wreck, smoke rising like a funeral pyre in the bright sunshine. But she was dead. Only the pilot could have survived.

Shouts rang out from the trenches.

"Yow. Wow-wow-wow. Yow. Wow-wow-wow."

I raised my head above the grass. Brasso was yelping and dancing like a Red Indian, steel flashing in his hand. But his joy was short lived.

"Get your head down you daft sod!"

Small-arms fire cracked from the area of the sheds below us. He ducked back down behind the blocks of peat forming the trench's crude parapet. Another few shots rang out. No sign of the intended target. No hiss of disturbed air or spurt of shale? Where the hell were the bastards? I squinted through the grasses examining the jumble of sheds. A telltale puff of smoke would do.

But there was nothing – not a movement.

Seconds passed, then the waiting was broken.

"Jesus Christ. The daft bastards!" It was Brum, his voice urgent.

I looked across to his trench, then followed his line of vision. Adrenalin pumped. There was movement now. The enemy were out in the open. Hidden from the bank of trenches on our right by the sheds, the party dropped by the Alouette was advancing along the beach towards the helipad – directly into our 'killing field'.

From their positions amongst the sheds they would have seen the fire coming from the plateau on our right. The poor sods had no idea that we would guard the obvious line of approach. Whoever trained them should have been hung.

I hollered the command simultaneously with Pete Leach.

"Don't just bleeding look at 'em. SHOOT THE FUCKERS!"

The air was ripped violently apart. The gun jumped in Brum's hands, eager to hurl its death load into the oncoming Argentine Marines, snatching, chewing up and spitting out smoking cartridge shells in a hail of bone-smashing lead.

It had been sighted to perfection.

The beach was a slaughterhouse. Three bodies were thrown back with his first sweep. Bits flying off them. Weapons tossed from their hands. The spared ones dropped low and bolted for cover, tracer flicking behind them as Brum brought the GPMG back round. Legs disappeared behind the nearest shed. Bullets lashed through its timber corner, splinters flying, showing white under the dark paintwork, and they'd gone.

The silence rang. Smoke rose from the GPMG. Brum put his hand behind his neck and eased his shoulders. "Should keep them a bit quieter."

I picked up the sound of spent shells rattling in the bottom of the trench as he moved his feet.

But the quiet was not to last. The big noise had returned, drifting away then increasing, ominous, unseen, from behind the cliff face. I placed it fast. It was the Guerrico, her predator's bow emerging once more from behind the screen of rocks.

"Here she comes lads." But this time she was moving slower; maybe only a few knots.

"Arrogant bastards." I heard Jock snap in another clip.

She came out steady, twenty, thirty, fifty feet – her 100mm gun once again swinging round towards the shore.

But this time it was business. She was back for revenge.

A cloud of smoke left the recoiling barrel. A sound like an express train roared overhead, followed by an explosion as the shell smashed into the mountainside above Shackleton House. Around the bay the mountains joined in the game, the sound crackling from crag to crag like thunderbolts in a lightening storm. Whoosh. Another, lower down, hammered into the scree.

She hove into the bay, gradually leaving the concealment of the cliff face, firing shell after shell. 260 feet in and her tail left the cover of the rocks. Then the Bofors swung, yawed, and opened up, barrels pulsing like pistons in the bright sun. Somehow they had guessed our position. Maybe the survivors from the first party had comms.

Brum's machine gun hammered back, lead spat from my SLR. They'd see us now by the gas from the reload chambers and the tracer. The grass buzzed and sighed around me, then a noise like a jackhammer on overtime hit the house, punching a line of fist-sized holes through the dark green wall.

I heard a jarring impact on the shale to the left, ground my body down into the turf, then it came again. Only lower. Closer. Wasps plucked at my windproof, some slamming into the trench parapet. Then back again, lower, thud, thud, thud, deep into the face of the ridge.

Shit and grass filled the air obscuring the sun.

Whump, whump came from the ground beneath me. The trench had got it again. Then the hammering stopped and my neck crawled with dirt and debris sticking to the sweat as the air cleared around us.

"CEASE FIRING!" came screaming across the track from Mills.

We fell silent. The Guerrico steamed on. The Bofors stuttered, drilling lines a little further down, sending up great clouds of choking dust and fragments of broken scree. The crew had now lost the little puffs of telltale smoke that gave away our positions – maybe they thought we were all dead.

I watched, mesmerised. Walking pace, her bow wave just a ripple, the sleek grey shape came closer, she was still not fully alongside us.

"Come on then, you bastard." drifted through the grasses. The bofors raked back again, peppering the house, the sound of smashing glass joining the murderous onslaught. Another shell flashed and burst on the mountain wall.

I raised my head. Across the water a chopper had set down near the distant cemetery enclosure, black shapes dropped, then slipped away fast into cover. Still the Warship closed, bofors belching flame, slamming lead into the shale pile behind the trenches on my right.

Sweat tingled on my spine. Mouth dry, I echoed the call from the trench. Yeah come on, you arrogant fucker.

"Wait for it lads" came the shout.

The front bridge windows became oblique and The Guerrico's flank slipped along until she was parallel with my vision. She was as close to the shore as the channel allowed. She could come no nearer. She was directly alongside our positions.

"FIRE!!!" Screamed out.

Mills had timed it to perfection.

The gates of hell had swung wide and the ship was in.

Neat adrenalin pumped through my veins.

Every weapon on the plateau let loose a hail of British fury, smashing like a hundred rivet guns into the aluminium flank of the mighty ship.

Her head was in our noose. The giant front-mounted gun swung and traversed uselessly.

I pumped half a magazine through the windows on the side of the bridge. A short burst from her Bofors thumped under my body, lifting the ground, sending up a cloud of choking debris.

I wiped grit from my eyes and raised my head, levelling my sights again.

Brasso was feverishly ripping open ammo boxes. The snake of Brum's ammo belt jumped and writhed as he held sustained bursts. Tracer after tracer disappeared deep into the belly of the trapped leviathan.

My finger caressed the trigger. Five, six more rounds into the Exocet launchers. I thumbed sweat and muck from the corner of my eye and repositioned my rifle.

Bodies rose across the track. I slammed in another clip. The torsos of Dave Combes and John Stonestreet had emerged through the haze of smoke.

Combes had the Carl Gustav 84mm tank-busting rocket launcher on his shoulder, its stand hanging limp at his chest, one hand on the front grip, the other wrapped around the pistol grip. John cracked the venturi chamber shut, inches behind Dave's right ear and dropped on one knee. From all around them, sustained gunfire slammed into the armour plating of the spitting Bofors. Combes raised the drainpipe barrel, head tucked in tight to the iron sights.

Waited, still as a statue.

Pull the trigger for Christ's sake!

Flame roared from the venturi and the missile left the rifled tube in a frenzy of tortured light. My eyes followed the deadly warhead, streaking up, high into the blue sky across the frozen sunlit brine.

The ship was maximum range and moving, but Combes was an expert.

Coming down in a shallow arc, the Swedish armour-piercing rocket sliced wickedly into the hull, punching a gaping hole in her dull grey plates.

"YES!"

A deep booming explosion shook the vessel from bow to stern. Indian war whoops and triumphant cheers joined the smoke and grit hanging like a low cloud in the mild Antarctic air. I closed my left hand around the familiar wooden grip and rested the warm stock against my cheek.

Another noise cut through – familiar, deadly.

The rush of a 66mm rocket fizzed and rushed, corkscrewing over the helipad towards the ship. Nige Peters had released one of his LAWs. It sped towards the Guerrico like a skyrocket out of control, slamming into the gap between the giant weight of the heavily armoured forward gun and the steel plate beneath, exploding in ear-splitting fury. The gun bucked, swivelled and stopped, its barrel fixed on the sky in a rictus of death.

Through the smoke I watched John Stonestreet coolly sliding another rocket into the Carl Gustav. The Bofors hammered viciously around the two men, grass and shit flying everywhere. He slammed shut the venturi, dropped to the side, hands clasped over ears, close in to Dave's legs. The warship steamed on, her death blow imminent. I lowered my sights.

Waited.

Nothing happened.

Combe's mouth opened, the breach mounted recoil damper still tucked tight against his shoulder, and he was shouting. It was a misfire!

John leaped up ... what the fuck was he doing? He threw open the venturi, fingers grasping, heaved out the live missile, tossed it into the tussock grass and reached down for a replacement.

The big ship steamed on.

John thrust in another round, powerful hands twisting the long blue warhead into place. Dropped again. My pulse pounded. Combes took careful aim.

Thump, thump, thump.

I counted the beats.

This time? We still had her.

Nothing.

Shit! Another dud!

Surely he'd leave it? Once triggered, the charge could go off at any time. It would wipe them from the face of the plateau.

But in a frenzy, they tried again. Fingers tearing at the catch, Stonestreet, heaved out the charged warhead, threw it like a discarded toy over the grassy slope, and hauled up the next.

But once again it was a misfire.

"Shit!"

Stonestreet left it, and the two men dropped out of sight.

My mouth was dry and felt like the bottom of a birdcage.

I put more angry rounds into the riddled hull and watched her sail slowly out of the Carl Gustav's range. Four out of our five 84mms spent, and three of them useless.

Dust and diesel smoke choked in the air, biting a rush of acid bile into my sinuses.

Bollocks! We had just one rocket left.

Zip, zip. Two bullets whipped through the grass. Close, like summer gnats. Sporadic fire, rifle and automatic, was coming up from the sheds.

Brum's GPMG stuttered back.

Splinters flew. Windows smashed inwards. Glinting shards like sharks teeth, grinned back from the shattered frames.

I raised my sights and looked along them towards the Guerrico. The great ship had reached the tip of King Edward Point, her white bow wave obscured behind the sheds.

Above her oblique superstructure, across the crystal water, I watched an Alouette settle by the stricken Puma. Another rose into the blue from the cemetery, dipped its nose and raced back along Brown Mountain Ridge, a black carrion crow against the white snowy crags.

Foam kicked from the Leviathan's stern, and the Bofors crew swung the heavy armour plating toward the trenches on our main ridge. Flame licked from the pulsing barrels as the weapon traversed towards its target.

Then, a flash of orange Mae West caught my eye.

I could see a gunner.

The weapon swivelled further.

Stupid fuckers. They were now in our sights and stood out like nuns in a brothel.

Chubb and Parsons, high up to the east, on the ridge under Shackleton's cross, must have thought it was Christmas. Tracer flicked past my line of vision, a vicious hose of light spraying out across the gap, red-hot stars against the white of the ridge.

Thunder followed the light.

I pictured the wicked barrel of the long black LMG, kicking eagerly on its bipod, as the two Marines brought it round to bear on the stern of the warship.

Legendary and deadly accurate over vast distances, the British gun did its worst. Tracer snaked behind the armour, three bullets to every white-hot ball, it dealt its lethal payload. Orange bodies flew out, dancing like puppets. I lowered my SLR and watched them drop. No more now than bright twisted shapes, sprawled unnaturally on the dull grey deck.

The gun fell silent.

Shouts and cheers rang out from the trenches.

The Guerrico steamed on.

She dragged herself behind the huts, obscuring the gaping hole in her side, and made her way past the Point to begin her turn in the broad deep pool of Grytviken Harbour.

Good. She had no option now but to try to escape.

Brasso hollered like a Comanche.

My blood was up and I felt the broad grin twisting my jaw.

Leopard-crawling across the ground, I dropped flat beside the trench, then slid over the lip amongst the spent tubes. Single shots from the Argentine Marines below us zipped through the grass, finding the green wall of the house.

"Welcome to our happy home." Brum spat on the barrel of his GPMG. The saliva sizzled with the heat. He pulled a sympathetic face at the crouching figure next to him. Beret pulled firmly down, Brasso was ripping at the ammunition boxes in the bottom of the trench. He slammed a lid shut and bobbed up.

"Getting low, Brum. I'll haul some back from the dump."

He put a hand on each side of the trench, making to clamber up to ground level. Blood stained his fingers.

"Shit. Let's have a look Brasso lad." I grabbed a wrist and turned his hand over. His fingers were blistered and raw. Brum had been putting full rounds through the ravenous gun – usually only used in five-second bursts. Brasso had been linking in the clips as they flew from the belt boxes, red-hot spent cylinders crashing around him.

"Alright, I'll pop and see nurse while I'm at it." He grinned. "That's as long as Pete don't get me with another fucking window." He pulled himself up over the side of the pit and slipped back towards the house.

"How many you reckon are down there?" I nodded towards the huts.

"Can't be sure." Brum rubbed muck off his forehead.

"Could be bleeding dozens of the bastards by now." Jesse swept an armful of smoking shells from the parapet. "Been coming in by chopper on our blind spot, behind the radio hut." He pointed to where we'd seen flashing blades between the timber buildings. As if to confirm his take, the stutter of a machine gun rattled up towards us, sending a spray of shale debris from the loose pile just above the trenches on the main ridge.

"It's not them we should worry about. It's the guys in the town that'll give us the problems." I nodded towards the cemetery – more figures had appeared.

"There's another lot, on their way now."

Just over 1000 yards away across the water another helicopter had lifted off, figures going to ground swiftly among the neat white gravestones of the town's cemetery.

The rusted hulk of a whaler lay half submerged just beyond, between the enemy and the town. It afforded vital cover. Bodies ducked and weaved forward, kept low by the constant withering fire directed on them from our northernmost trenches on the main plateau.

Still they came on, determined, purposeful, closing in from the north, finally reaching cover, hidden from view by the ruined outlying tin shacks of the capital.

I dragged my eyes away and narrowed them towards the distant valley. It ran up at a steep gradient between the snowy mountains behind the little church. If we could battle our way out past the sheds below us, and along the exposed track towards Grytviken, then the dip between the peaks would be our escape route.

Not like we had a choice, there was no other way out.

On our left, just past Shackleton's Monument, the land fell into the sea. Behind us was the shallow scree pile, then solid rock covered in snow rising 500 feet into the blue – nigh on impossible to climb. If we tried it in daylight we'd be picked off like flies on a whitewashed wall. Ahead of us, nothing but the frozen Antarctic waters of the southern seas.

Crunching on the brass tubes littering the peat floor of the trench, I moved into the V shaped point where Brasso had been working the belts. The bridge of my boot had come down on something less giving than the shells. Moving my foot, I squinted down into the shadow of the wet peat. Below me the red handle of the fire axe and gleaming plate of its broad head lay ready for action, beneath the litter of dull brass.

Sustained automatic enemy fire came from the northwest, and across the stretch of water enemy troops raced from cover to cover between the rusting factories lining Grytviken harbour. A figure flitted across the narrow lane where the Russian spy ship had laid her pipes, then another followed, moving fast. If you blinked you'd miss them. Shit. They were cutting us off fast. In twenty minutes they'd reach the church.

Grass parted and Brasso slid back into the trench, dragging boxes. He hadn't gone un-noticed. Two or three bullets zipped past, like angry gnats, one ricocheting at the end of its journey from the rocks behind the house.

"Right Jesse," I grinned down at Brasso's back, watching him purposefully piling the ammo up in the bottom of the trench. "Best make ready with the mortar, in case they make a move and get to the nearest sheds. We'll use smoke first, then HE"

Jesse smiled, mouth closed, eyeing up the distance. "It's just about the limit of our range but we should be able to lob one in from here."

All the while, the Guerrico had been constantly on the move. Slowly her razor bow had turned in the pool of the deep harbour, circling out towards Brown Mountain, as far away from our puny weapons as she could sail. First port side on to the rusting dockside, before facing us head on, showing her sleek predator lines, until her port side had swung obliquely into view and she was facing the channel once again.

She was in clear view now, maybe 750 yards away. But would she stay or try to leave? If it was the latter, then she would need to pass King Edward Point, which would once again hide her briefly behind the jumble of tin sheds, before she came into full view again in the narrow deep channel, close in to our positions. It was the route she must take to reach the cover of the rocks once more at Hope Point – her only way out.

But she appeared to have stopped dead. She was stationary in the water – not a sign of movement. So what the hell would she do now? Every one around me watched and waited.

Minutes ticked slowly by, then came a white ribbon of movement in the water at her bows and it was clear to us that the captain had made his decision. The warship was beginning to move in our direction. She was off...

Black smoke belched from her funnel. The captain either had balls, or was a fucking idiot, but he had made his decision. The Guerrico would run our gauntlet.

Feet pounded behind me. Pete Leach's broad back melted into the shadow of the long green house.

Ammunition mags rattled and snapped through the grass.

The Guerrico's captain gave her full clog. White foam boiled. Her stern dropped and the bow began to eat water.

On she came, into our maelstrom of lead. Every 'small arm' on the northwest ridge hammered out a renewed hail of lead, peppering her hull and superstructure with a thousand lacerations as she powered towards us.

Behind and above me Pete Leach had taken position with his sniper's rifle, just inside the glassless corner window of the house. Above the thunder of our weapons came the sound of his L42's free-floating barrel, barking its deadly song.

The front port window of the fleeing warship disappeared, the sound of smashing glass penetrating the roar of our onslaught.

Crack! Followed by the thump of impact! Death left the barrel again.

The next window flew inwards like the last.

Pete could put a hole in the centre of a man's forehead at 1000 yards.

Inside the bridge would be carnage.

Her bow sliced behind the tin huts of the point.

She was doing thirty, spewing great clouds of diesel smoke, laying it behind like a cloak. White water, spraying high in rainbow droplets, leapt from her forward plates.

For a few seconds she was almost completely obscured from view. Then the high bow wave reappeared from behind the tin shacks, flat out, going for broke, into the channel between the two points and she was alongside once more. Belching black fury, her diesels were screaming like a wounded sea monster, screws torturing the frozen brine in a bubbling storm of panic.

My shoulder pumped with the action of my SLR emptying the chamber into her flank.

Another mag – where the fuck is it? – slammed in.

Whack, whack. More lead through the bridge side window.

Above the thunderstorm of flying lead, the rivet gun noise had kicked back in with a vengeance. Like a hundred hammers beating out a tuneless tattoo, the noise of striking bullets and shattered glass came back to us through the murderous din.

Thump. Crash. Another pane fell from the house behind us. The L42 barked again, but nearer to me now – Pete had moved position.

We poured in more lead.

The Guerrico bellowed on, the stench of warfare hanging low, choking.

I dragged a sleeve across my eyes and caught a familiar movement over the track. There, through the smoke, blinding flashes and puffs of ejector gas, was Combes – as cool as before, Carl Gustav rock solid on his shoulder, our last killer punch in the tube.

"GO ON MY SON!"

The drainpipe barrel bucked into the haze.

Flame shot from the venturi, past Stonestreet's left shoulder. The thunderbolt left the tube in a roar of smoke and sparks. Transcending the noise of our puny weapons the Carl Gustav 84mm savaged the air like an avenging Valkyrie, winging across the sky in relentless pursuit.

The Guerrico was going like an express train. But there was no escape.

The armour-piercing rocket slammed into the sinister twin Exocet launcher, abaft the funnel, exploding in a flash of white light and a noise like rolling thunder.

"YES!"

She bucked and shuddered like a live animal.

Bloodlust was up. Neat adrenalin hammered through my veins. Banshee shouts and Red Indian war cries filled the choking air. But still the Guerrico hammered on. Listing to starboard. Grey smoke curled and licked down her side, then trailed behind with her belching diesel exhaust, mixing and swirling into the great valley of her foaming wake.

Below me, amongst the sheds, pinpoints of automatic fire and telltale flashes of ejector gas drummed out a warning. Lead zipped past, raddling the timber thirty feet behind me like a demented woodpecker.

A GPMG from the furthest trench hammered back, cutting a swathe of death through the nearest hut. Glass, tin and splinters, filled the air. A cloud of dust rose like smoke, hiding the alleyways and drifting into the shadows.

Clip empty, I dropped the gritty timber stock from my cheek and snatched up a replacement. Air rushed above my beret. A line of bullet holes ripped into the house, zip fastener straight, running up the wall at a 45 degree angle.

A boot hit a window just feet away from the new scar. The pane flew out, seemed to hang in the air, flashed in the sun, dropped, and shattered on the glass-littered shale path beneath. The noise of impact joined the firestorm – Pete Leach was following the ship in her path of flight.

Snap, clip in, I brought the rifle back to the side of my face.

The Guerrico's speed was terrific. She was closing fast now on the shelter of Hope Point rocks.

Two more shots in quick succession sang out from the upper floor of the house.

Then, flank full onto the monument ridge, Chubby and Parsons had her once more full in their sights. Armour piercing tracer poured into her hide, joining our ribbons of stars, hosing through the acrid smoke that was belching and obscuring her foaming stern.

Still she motored on.

The great curl of her bow wave finally reached the crag and slid like a scimitar behind the steel grey cliff face.

In seconds the rest of her had dragged itself in and behind, and all we were left with was the foul smell of diesel exhaust, the crash of her wake on the shore, and the cloud of her passage settling low onto the icy pool of Grytviken harbour.

I reached into my webbing, found my flask, took a pull, swilled round and spat out. The Guerrico had come in roaring like a lion, a complete modern warship, with enough hardware to take out a town.

She was now no more than a floating wreck.

I pulled back from the parapet of the ridge, away from the trajectory of intermittent enemy fire, still dribbling up from the sheds, and jinked through the tough grass to the edge of the trench. The quiet between the pops and cracks of small arms, whined its tinnitus whistle loud in my ears.

On my right, guys were moving about urgently on the main ridge.

I dropped down next to the damp pit.

"Don't knock then." Jesse looked up, running his sleeve along the black plastic stock of his rifle.

"Fuck off. Everyone alright?" I scanned around.

I could see they were.

Jesse licked his thumb and forefinger and began to carefully clean his front site.

Brasso grinned, pulling up the great axe from under a thick pile of spent cartridges, some still smoking.

Brum squinted up from the machine gun, eased his neck, looked across at me and nodded. "Yeah, we're OK, Nige Peters ain't though, old son."

"Fuck." I dropped my grin. "Bad?"

"Bad enough. Word came across the track just now. Fucking only stood up with that bleeding 66mm rocket launcher, just after Combesy whacked the bastard. Belgian automatic they reckon. He took two through his upper arm. Smashed to fucking bits."

"Shit."

"Yeah."

I narrowed my eyes at him. "Morphine?"

"Keep him going for a bit won't it?" He shook his head.

"Aye. That's about all."

Field dressings, morphine, a rudimentary understanding of first aid, and that was it. I pictured our escape route. It would be torture for him.

"Christ. If it's as bad as you say, the poor sod needs a doc' quick."

Eight thousand miles from home – fat chance.

"Tell me about it." It was Brasso. "If he don't get it, and we make a run for it, he won't last more than a few days." He wiped his chin with the back of his hand. "When the morphine runs out the pain'll fucking kill him."

Nobody spoke for a few seconds.

"If that don't... the bloody gangrene will," Jesse said quietly, looking up from his work. He wasn't smiling.

Didn't have to spell it out. The shit in the wound wouldn't go away without medical care. We all knew it. Gangrene was a bastard way to die.

There was still not even a breeze to stir the stalks around us, or to brush the surface of the harbour waters. In no time the deep pool had slipped back to its impersonation of an azure blue mirror, as though the ship had been no more than a nightmare mirage. Even the stench of her exhaust had begun to settle, seeping like a ghost into the grit and the rock.

The smell of the sea and kelp began to faintly permeate back through the grasses again, a backdrop scent – and a welcome one – to the stench of cordite and ejector gas.

The scene flickered in my peripheral vision, bringing my focus up and across to the far side of the harbour waters. Skimming along the line of Brown Mountain Ridge, another chopper appeared, the sound of her rotors echoing faintly in and out of earshot across the bay.

It was another drop.

Throughout the conflict they had been scurrying back and forth, dropping off heavily armed assault troops, like extras in a crowd scene, playing second fiddle to the main event.

Indistinct shouting drifted from the right hand trenches.

The Alouette was making for the same spot – the cemetery again.

She slowed and put down.

A cry sang out from my right.

Men dropped from the chopper and a barrage of rifle fire from the trenches on the main ridge split the air like crackling thunder.

I lowered my SLR and followed suit, aiming high and a few feet in front of the darting figures. They had to be fifteen hundred yards away, but in the absence of any other targets it would have to do. 'If we can just pin them down 'til nightfall' ran in my head over and over like a scratched record.

Whatever the plan, no way were they going to attempt to storm the thousand yards of exposed path running along the side of the bay, between our positions and the capital.

For that matter neither were we.

No. For now, keep them holed up in the ruins of the town and deal with the events as they unfold. However, one thing we could be fairly sure of was that it was unlikely that they would be coming for us now, either by air or by sea.

Narrowing my eyes, I scanned across the body littered foreshore, to the smoking pile of the helicopter gunship on the far bank, then out through the mouth of the bay towards the Guerrico. She had reappeared from behind the rocks of Hope Point, listing to starboard and about half a mile out to sea.

A mile behind her and to one side, the *Bahia Paraiso* still lay watching, as she had throughout the conflict. The Alouette, having left the ridge, was now a tiny dot and closing in on her fast. I looked away and turned my attention back to the tell tale ghosts of smoke emitting from the deep shadows between the distant rusting buildings. I raised my sights, took careful aim, then the thunderbolt struck.

The express train was back. Ripping the air asunder, a shell roared overhead, smashing into the mountain wall, high up with ear-splitting fury, echoing and crackling back from the white crags enclosing the bay. Blinding light, debris and smoke rumbled down the edifice.

Cries and shouts of "COVER!" drifted through deafened ears.

I found it hard to focus.

"Shit!"

"What the fuck!"

Shouts mingled as one.

Jesse tugged my sleeve and pointed.

Out to sea, a pinprick of light and smoke illuminated the Guerrico's crippled front gun.

"Shit. She's bleeding shelling us! I thought we'd banjaxed the bastard!"

Howling demons rent the air. Lower. Four high explosive shells jack-hammered deep into the rock face. Stone rained down, clattering onto the roof of the big house, grit landing amongst us like hail.

"But the bleeding gun's jammed." Brum raised his eyes above the parapet.

"Yeah," Jesse spat out, "but look at the bastards. Look what they're fucking doing."

"Bollocks."

The Guerrico was on the move. Her stern boiling white water as she dragged herself further out to sea.

"They're going to fucking shunt the wreck around till they've got our range, ain't they?" Jesse's face wore a grim smile. "Those first shots will give them a bearing, I reckon. Then once they get it right," he squinted across the sunlit water at the manoeuvring warship, "they'll be dropping em' right on fucking top of us."

Minutes went by, punctuated by the crack of small arms from the point and the whirr of the distant Alouette, once again on its way back along the snow capped ridge.

The Guerrico had stopped dead in the frozen water again.

I watched, fascinated. Jesse had guessed her intentions. The bastards were determined.

Bright flashes of light left her forward gun.

"DOWN!"

Armour-piercing shells tortured the air. They hammered overhead at arms reach, above the ridge, missed the house and struck home into the solid wall of rock, four in a row, twenty feet lower than the first shells. Adrenalin pumped – thump thump in my ears – to the violence of the multiple thunderclap. Sound drifted away to silence, then came clamouring back, screaming through my head, like a thousand alarm bells.

Smoke and dust choked the air.

In slow motion the ringing in my head dissipated and the atmosphere began to clear around us. Through the haze, I watched the crippled ship as she yawed, ultra-slowly across to port, white water boiling from her props, then carefully begin to ease about. Her movements were calculated, purposeful and sinister. Whoever was now in command was taking their time, making ready for another salvo.

Indistinct shouting sounded from the grasses thirty feet behind the trench. Someone was trying to call a message up to Pete Leach. The Sergeant Major's voice came back through the shattered building behind me, then seconds later a door crashed open and his parade ground yell sounded from the porch.

"COVERING FIRE!" bellowed above the rattle of an enemy automatic.

Keeping low, the heavy L42 in his fist, Pete jinked across the track towards Mills' trench. Brum's machine gun kicked eagerly. Lead spat from every weapon on both ridges.

This would be it then. Mills must need to discuss our next move.

Four more shells hurtled overhead.

"Right Jesse lad!" I shouted over the din. "I reckon it's time we put some mortars in."

I nodded down to the cluster of buildings nearest the jetty.

Muzzle flashes from Belgian automatics had been getting closer, steadily moving up through the sheds. They were close enough now. Hopefully, all in the vicinity of the nearest buildings. A mortar amongst them should achieve maximum damage with one salvo.

I heaved the short black tube up from where it lay beside its casing in the wet grass, ran a finger round the inside of the rim and calculated the trjectory. The '2 inch' had a maximum killing range of around 300 yards. But the sheds were less than half that distance.

The sound of boots thumped through the grass behind me, and I turned from setting up the directory of the tube to see Pete hammering back towards the porch.

Jesse piled out a couple of 900 gram smoke and a pile of heavier high explosive bombs. Smoke would get us our range, then onto rapid fire – we could sling them down at eight rounds a minute.

"READY!" I shouted. Automatic fire zipped overhead, smashing splinters from the corner of the house.

Jesse raised his head again, jaw clamped shut, and grinned evilly across.

Kneeling – tube dug in – angled just off the vertical towards the point – left hand fingers wrapped around the black steel, I lifted the smoke canister – brought it up to the tube then stopped abruptly at a shout that had come from somewhere behind me. I spun round to see that it was Pete Leach.

"Whoa!" He yelled from the corner window of the house. "You'll fucking hit Mills!"

Then more shouting came to my ears, drifting across from the main ridge, and all around us the sound of gunfire abruptly ceased.

"What?" I dropped my arm and rested the base of the smoke bomb on a patch of shale between the tussocks. What the hell was going on? "Where is he, then?"

"Down there." The big man angled his head towards the slope below us. My eyes traversed the battleground and caught a movement to the right. Mills, SMG strapped across his back, came into view, walking purposefully, dead centre down the puddled track past the bungalow-shaped building nearest our ridge.

"What the fuck!"

He left the cover, stepped out into the open killing ground at a steady pace, and kept walking.

Every head on the plateau turned towards the lone figure. No sound of movement left the trenches; not even a breeze rustled the tall grass. The silence dropped down around us under a heavy cloak of unreality.

Seconds crawled past.

The diminishing figure came level with the helipad. He walked on without a glance, passing its crumbling sheet of concrete and stepped on into the final hundred yards of stony outcrop that separated him from the deadly cluster of sheds on the point.

He couldn't have.

I looked round at Pete. Shook my head. "Tell me he hasn't?"

"He fucking has!" Leach's eyes shone down from the gaping hole of the window, like angry black coals. "He's only gone and bleeding jacked it in already."

I felt my mouth hanging open and clamped it shut. Realisation of Pete's reply hit home, like a physical blow.

"Bollocks. We're six nil up! Winning hands down, man."

The distant figure of Lieutenant Mills disappeared amongst the clutter of sheds.

Pete nodded, his eyes drilling me across the gap, a slit of a smile above his powerful jaw. "I know. But he's the boss, George. His decision. We go along with it." Shifting his big frame from the opening, he moved back into the shadow of the room and disappeared once more into the darkness of the pockmarked house.

A string of expletives erupted from the trench.

Adrenalin still flowed like blood.

The warrior spirit was up.

To end it now seemed like a betrayal.

I laid the tube of the mortar back down in the grass, next to its gaping case, and handed Jesse the smoke bomb. He took it with a wry smile, shaking his head, breathing heavily down his nose.

Fragmented emotions banged around in my skull.

Five minutes clawed by, lead-heavy with silence, before Mills reappeared, surrounded by Argies. He stood in the open, away from the deep shadows between the sheds, surreal in the sunshine, signalling with both arms for us to come down.

Stunned seconds ticked... The message kicked in – he'd done it.

"Jesus Christ! Is that poxing it then!?" Brum spat the words.

Jesse and Brasso scowled down the track, cursing.

"Fucking looks like it," I nodded, anger and resentment boiling. "Best head off. Get yourselves down there."

I tried to focus on what we were being ordered to do. A feeling of unreality swam around in my senses. This couldn't be happening.

Some of our guys were already on the gravel track, closing in on the nearest building. Jock walked by shaking his head. Jesse and Brum, grim faced, clambered out of the pit and followed.

Brasso was the last to leave. "See you down there George." There was no grin.

He heaved himself up to ground level, his Arctic windproof hanging open.

Two hand axes flashed from his webbing like a sharp-shooter's handguns. He'd meant what he said... I'd never doubted him.

I peered down into the shadow of the trench wall. The giant fire axe reclined in the sharp front corner by the spent ammo boxes. There was no sign of the wet peat forming its floor. Just a carpet of empty brass shells.

Porter, Church and Daniels joined the thin speckled line, dropping down the curved slope towards the level ground of the foreshore. Their shadows marched before them. Twice their height in the early low sun, pointing like dark accusing fingers, arrow straight towards the ruined capital, Grytviken.

"Oi! Anything been happening while we've been away?" The unmistakeable sound of Chubb's voice broke into my thoughts. He was walking past the house with Steve Parsons, running his fingers over the craters and bullet holes.

"Not a lot."

"Typical. We've been fighting a fucking war up there, while you dozy lot have been day-dreaming."

"Wondered what the noise was." I tried to force a grin, but my face would have cracked.

The trademark low laugh drifted down. "Course you did. Can't stop. Got to run. Shall I tell our new friends to expect you?" He inclined his head and spat towards the foreshore, where dozens of Argentine Special Assault Troops were lining up the men.

"Yeah." My eyes dragged back to the beach, still unable to believe what was happening. "Bastards. Get the beer on ice, man."

Boots scrunching on the glass and loose shale, the two Marines headed for the track.

The door of the dark green house opened and closed, clicking heavily on its weatherproof catch. The noise drew me round to peer into the darkness of the porch. With Chubb and Parsons gone I'd thought I was alone, but a shadow moved and Pete Leach walked out into the sunshine.

"All gone, George?" Tiger bright eyes glared past me at the line of Royal Marines gathering on the beach.

"Aye. Chubb and Parsons have just gan' down." Their heads disappeared below the level of the plateau as they dropped down the steep incline towards the level track.

"Well, best we make a move then, get it over with." He forced the corners of his mouth up, then pulled a bottle of spirits from each of his side pockets. "Come on, things are never that bad." He continued, "time to go home."

I watched his broad back as he crunched off across the shattered window panes, leaving me alone on the ridge.

Then a movement caught my eye. It was the bow wave from a landing craft, flashing in the sunshine as it ploughed through the frozen water, rounding Hope Point. Black Argy helmets showed above the high sides. The boat then turned and began to close on our spit of land. With the ceasefire in operation the reinforcements in the troop carrier would be heading towards the easiest place to disembark – and that would be the low square jetty.

I left it to its steady approach and lowered my eyes to the promontory of land spread out below me. On the landward side of the jetty, Argentine troops, dropped by chopper during the battle, appeared from the tight cluster of sheds and began to mass on the foreshore of the stony beach.

"Shit."

On cue, a new chill breeze stirred from nowhere and began to pick at the long grass. I swore, pulled up my collar and made to leave.

Then another movement dragged my eyes down.

In front of me, two feet below the parapet of the trench, hung the white plastic double light switch.

Suspended by its tangle of coloured wires, it was swinging... gently, enticingly, a hair's breath from the blood-red handle of the great axe.

The switch held the power of life and death. One flick and the deadly payload of harpoon heads and scrap iron, wrapped around our hidden mines, would blow the landing craft out of the water and cut down the enemy on the beach, like a scythe through corn.

Fuck it!

If I used it now there would be indiscriminate carnage. Our guys were down there too. A cold blast buffeted in, chucking a cloud across the sun's face. The colour drained from the land.

I laid my rifle down in the tall grass and began the long walk down.

EPILOGUE

Unseen from our position, Mills, using the long barrel of an SLR, had waved his windproof, turned inside out so that the white webbing showed, above his trench before heading down to the sheds on King Edward Point.

He'd carefully worked out the odds.

Apart from the fact that the Argentine troops, dropped into Grytviken, outnumbered us many times to one, they had also cut us off from the only escape route, past the little church.

In theory, despite the odds, we could have taken them on at close quarters amongst the ruins, and made a dash for the valley behind. But in order to engage them, we'd have had to cross the 1000 yards of open ground first.

That way was suicide.

The truth was, though, that if we didn't, it was only a matter of time before the crippled Guerrico got her range. It seemed certain to the Lieutenant that she would. After all, he reasoned, she had all day and the shells were creeping closer and closer to our positions.

So that was it, then. Mills had indeed called for a ceasefire. It was a brave decision and, looking back, the right one – an action for which the Argentine commander, who met him on the point, was extremely grateful.

The lieutenant had risked his life by literally walking into the lion's den to deliver his ultimatum. It showed the professional quality of the Argy Marines that they held their fire during his long, lonely walk through the open killing fields. One twitchy trigger finger could have ended his brave action there and then.

Mills, once inside the cluster of huts on the point, was immediately surrounded by well-armed Special Assault Troops. Luckily the officer in charge spoke good English and Mills was able to deliver his ultimatum.

Mills told him the absolute truth, that we were well dug in and prepared to fight on to the last man. This would mean that many more Argentine troops would die if they attempted to dislodge us. However, if the guy agreed to guarantee us good treatment, we would be prepared to cease fighting and thus avoid any more casualties. The officer couldn't believe his luck and nearly shook the young Lieutenant's hand off.

What Mills didn't tell the Argentine commander, mind, was that the island's entire defence force only numbered twenty-two lightly armed Royal Marine Commandos and one of us was seriously wounded.

Well, Mills had played his trump card; it worked and a ceasefire was accepted.

Trouble was, though, after we'd all finally drifted down and they could only count twenty-two of us, they got decidedly twitchy. They thought it was a trap, fingers curled round triggers and where the hell were the bulk of our men? Mills had to work hard to convince them that what they saw was all there was. It didn't do their pride a bundle of good once they'd twigged it. The idea that just the few of us had totally stuffed them, slowly sunk in. Punching above your weight, wasn't in it. They gave us more room after that and kept their distance. But that wasn't the end of their anxiety.

Tension returned for our captors when they were informed about the booby traps. Les Daniels agreed to make these safe. Our guards watched with horror while he expertly defused the jetty alongside which they were moored, the mined beach under their feet, and the rigged-up sheds behind us. All of which had been lovingly laid by Les to strategically take out as many of them as possible.

Throughout our remaining time on the island the Argentine commander was as good as his word and we were treated well. A doctor arrived from the *Bahia Paraiso* to examine Nige Peters and later in the day, accompanied by the thirteen members of the British Antarctic Survey Team, we were taken out by landing craft to the big ship.

Before leaving the island, Mills and Leach had been allowed back into Shackleton House to collect our small valuables. Any cameras they brought out were opened and the films destroyed. Mills' camera however, the one used to take the photo on the jetty, was not there, and survived intact. This was because Martin still had the camera on him when the shooting started. He had made a dash for a dip in the land and had lain, in just his shirtsleeves, suffering from the beginnings of hypothermia, hidden throughout. When he finally emerged, the camera was found but the guard, unable to work out how to open an Olympus OM10, gave up and allowed it to leave with us, the film still intact. This is how the iconic photo survives to this day.

A lot of our stuff stayed on the island as there wasn't time or space to take it. So the big Russian's bearskin hat became a spoil of war.

On our way out to the *Bahia Paraiso* we had sailed past the crippled Guerrico, but we never saw her close up. Our guard's macho South American pride had suffered enough. They were that upset that they took as wide a sweep round the listing ship as possible, so we couldn't admire our handywork.

We sailed that night and, after a quick call at Leith harbour, were soon headed out to sea, full speed ahead towards the Argentine mainland. Captain

Trombetta's priority was to get to the nearest hospital with the wounded troops. Earlier, the Argentine national hero and officer in charge of the military invasion, Teniente Alfredo Astiz, had flown in from the ship to speak to us while we were still ashore. Outwardly unruffled by the mauling of his invasion force, he congratulated us in perfect English on our defence of the island.

On board we met again and he took the opportunity to tell us that he thought all kamikaze hailed from Japan. Nice of him.

Strangely, after we came aboard, we found that we actually knew some of the Argentine Marines. Many of us had spent time in the resort of Mar Del Plata, which was near an Argentine Naval Base. We recognised them from the beaches and the bars and from military exercises. One guy reminded me that we'd met at a sergeants mess barbeque that summer! We'd got on well. It felt surreal that we knew these men and yet now we were at war.

After four days, we arrived off the coast of Tierra Del Fuego and docked at the port of Rio Grande. It was Captain Trombetta's first opportunity to off-load the casualties, including Nige Peters, to the nearby hospital.

Here at Rio Grande, we were incarcerated below deck and couldn't witness at first hand the activity going on above us, but heard helicopter after helicopter shuttling back and forth from ship to shore. We didn't need to see it, we knew how it worked. They would be ferrying the dead and the wounded. The rotors whirred non-stop for hour after hour. It brought it home to us. Our tiny force had exacted a fearful toll. But we were never told the score.

We sailed from Rio Grande, then six days later on the 13th of April, once again made landfall, this time at the naval base of Bahia Blanca. Here, we were taken ashore and from there ferried by bus to the naval camp's disused and drained swimming pool complex.

We were to spend the next four days inside this hastily converted building.
A film crew arrived on the first day and filmed us playing football, obviously for propaganda. Some of the guys even agreed to an interview.

On the second day we got a boost with the arrival back of Nige Peters. After initial treatment at Rio Grande, they had flown him up to Buenos Aires where surgeons had removed a bullet from his upper arm, before returning him back down south again to rejoin us.

On day three, unbelievably, an Argentine Admiral arrived to inspect us. Marching down the line he regarded us with great pride shaking us warmly by the hand treating us like we were some kind of returning national heroes. How weird was that? We'd fucked up one of his best ships and he thought we were great.

During our stay at the swimming pool complex, we were constantly being reassured that we were going home. Of course, we didn't believe it would happen, mind, and thought it to be a nasty, psychological game. Until day four, when the unbelievable actually happened, and they drove us out to an air-strip and put us on a plane for Montevideo, back where we started, in Uruguay.

Throughout our time as prisoners of Argentina, we were treated well. The reasoning behind their actions may have been because some of them could see the writing on the wall. That I don't know. But, whatever their reason, the message they were sending back could do them no harm.

When we touched down, it was to a heroes' welcome. Crowds of ex-pats and dozens of reporters and cameramen, representing the world's media, crammed into the reception hall. It was mind-blowing. We had no idea that the story of our return from South Georgia had become international news. We had to fight our way past the barrage of shouted questions, TV crews and flashlights, just to get to our transport.

Eventually, we were whisked away to one of Montevideo's most luxurious hotels, the Casino Carrasco, where we spent the next two nights. We were awake throughout, and the bar stayed open with us. We'd built up quite a thirst.

Finally, on April 20th, Mills led us down the steps of an RAF VC10 at RAF Brize Norton.

All nine of us from NP 8901 had returned, as had the detachment of Royal Marines from HMS *Endurance*, but not for long. In a few short days, many of us would find ourselves once again winging our way south into the storm, towards the battered skies and frozen waters of the southern hemisphere.

Back to the blood stained landscape of the South Atlantic War.

GLOSSARY

BAS	British Antarctic Survey
BFT	battle fitness test
Banjaxed	to ruin, to incapacitate
Barnet	barnet fair-hair
Beaver	De Havilland single prop seaplane
Bergen	rucksack used by the military
Bofors	20-40 mm automatic cannon
Bren gun	light machine gun
Cam shells	deflector doors at rear of jet engine which open to reverse the thrust of the exhaust
Camm'd	camouflaged
Clansman	radio system used by the British Military
Craic pronounced crack	fun, banter
Desert wellies	desert boots, suede high-sided comfortable boots
ETA	estimated time of arrival
Encryptograph machine	machine for encrypting and decrypting messages
GPMG	general purpose machine gun
Goffer waller	operator of a small shop or stand, usually unofficial
Harry black maskers	black masking tape; a valuable commodity
Heads	toilets
Head-over	soft green knitted tube, worn as scarf or pulled up to protect the head against extreme weather
HE	high explosives
LAW	light anti-tank weapon
Mag	magazine of rounds, ie ammunition
Matelot	sailor
OP	observation post
PE	plastic explosive
Pusser's	Royal Navy service issue, eg pusser's chariot (service issue bike)
Scran	food
Royals	Royal Marines
SLR	self loading rifle
Tannoy	Tannoy Ltd – a British manufacturer of loudspeakers and public address systems
Yomp	to force march with a heavy load
Wet	a drink of any description